"The right phrase should be – if you a
you should invest in planning. We
companies but when it comes to the f
then the only thing we seem to plan is a holiday. Jeremy Deedes has
written the most comprehensive explanation and guide for financial
planning I have ever read. More than that, though, he has made it
accessible and understandable for all."

**Justin Urquhart Stewart**
**Co-founder of Seven Investment Management**
**and financial commentator**

# RIGHT MONEY
# RIGHT PLACE
# RIGHT TIME

Personal finances to transform
your life and secure your future

## JEREMY DEEDES

# R3THINK PRESS

First published in Great Britain 2015
by Rethink Press (www.rethinkpress.com)

Illustrations by Tim Bulmer
Charts by Clang
Portrait photo: Tracey Phillips

# CONTENTS

# Introduction

## YOUR MONEY OR YOUR LIFE?

I have had the immense privilege over the last quarter of a century of working with clients in a deeply personal way to help them plan their finances, achieve their goals and sleep at night. Throughout those years I have learnt much from my clients and my professional colleagues, and I have developed a financial planning service that is truly client-centred and deals with money firmly in the context of life.

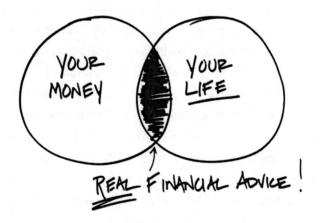

Financial planners have so much to offer to families and individuals struggling to deal with money on a day-to-day basis. Sadly, very few of those families take up that offer. We all know the reasons, which include distrust of financial services, fear of extortionate fees or commissions, a perceived lack of professionalism and a lack of faith in advisers to come up with the right solutions. There is also an ingrained and deeply-held assumption amongst consumers that they are fully capable of managing their own finances and don't need professional advice.

It is true that many families are competent at looking after their own money, although in the aftermath of the 2008 financial crisis we also know that many, many families got it very wrong and are now reaping the consequences of poor decisions. Sadly, it is often these men and women who end up seeking the help of the financial planning community.

So, the primary reason for this book is to help consumers become aware that there is a very real art and science to financial planning that can produce life-changing results for those who embrace the practice. I hope it will be of help to those who wish to retain their do-it-yourself approach to their finances, as well as those who understand that good financial planning advice is truly valuable and something to be embraced, not shunned.

Money is a very left-brain activity, centred on analysis and figures. It tends to be short-term and detailed, narrowly-focussed. Over the years the right brain, with a much broader view of life and its possibilities, has been side-lined in the financial services sector. Financial institutions have managed to divorce life from money over the years, concentrating on products rather than solutions, materialism rather than integrity, money as an end in itself rather than as a means to an end. In short, your money and *not* your life.

I am passionate about redressing this by taking a life first, money second approach. As you read the book you will swing between highly-focused, detailed, money-centred sections such as portfolio construction (left brain) and much less focused, outward-looking, life-centred chapters such as your personal projects (right brain). It is for this reason, to shift the emphasis back towards the outward-looking right brain that I begin with a wide-ranging overview of the world in which we live and work.

Having set the scene, I discuss the concept of planning in Chapter Two before looking at the life side of financial life planning in Chapters Three, Four and Five. Chapter Six addresses the day-to-day management of time and money, a chapter in which the *life* side of the plan and the *money* side come together. In Chapter Seven I introduce the concept of the three drivers of financial freedom and provide a model for a personal financial framework. Chapter Eight considers the true meaning of wealth. Chapters Nine and Ten look at implementing and renewing plans. I conclude in Chapter Eleven with a set of fundamental life and financial tenets, and a series of action steps for constructing and implementing your own financial plan.

The transition in the second half of the book from the softer, human side of money to the hard nuts and bolts of cash flow and investment management can be difficult. However, it is all part of the integrated, holistic planning process. It is important and needs as much attention as the preceding chapters.

Whilst I expect, and hope, that everyone reading this book will gain something from it I believe that the New Entrepreneurs who see their own business as an integral part of their drive for freedom will gain the most. These are the ever-increasing army of people, often working in the services sector, providing a range of solutions to niche and micro-niche markets and intent on building global small businesses on the back of their specialist intellectual property.

Although financial life planning is a process, I have avoided a straight-line, descriptive journey. It is more important to understand the key principles and concepts behind the process. Also bear in mind that this book is about planning, not products. Although my practice, Planning for Life, is authorised and regulated by the Financial Conduct Authority to provide investment advice, by far the largest element of my work with clients is to do with planning, visioning, cash flow, education and financial coaching, so you won't find detailed descriptions of financial products or tax-wrappers. There is a list of resources at the end of the book with sources of further information, if required.

The principles and processes of financial life planning can be applied by anyone wherever they live on the planet and I have tried to write this book for a global audience, reflecting the global presence of the financial planning community. However, regulatory regimes, tax regimes and financial products obviously differ from country to country. On occasions I have used examples from the UK to illustrate a point and it goes without saying that these may not apply if you live elsewhere.

Financial life planning has the potential to change your life – if you take action. To help you I have included short exercises in each chapter that can be done on the back of an envelope. Preparing and living your own plan is no small task. You will achieve more if you take it 'step by step' and completing these exercises as you read should make it easier to rise to the challenge of bringing your life and money back into harmony. Postscripts at the end of each chapter also add more depth to particular aspects of financial life planning.

So, please read on and happy planning.

# One

# RIDING THE FREEDOM TREND

'The past is a foreign country;
they do things differently there.'

L P HARTLEY

The world is more dynamic, less structured than it was only 20 years ago. Society and its values have changed. Technology has had, and continues to have, a huge impact on our personal, business and professional lives.

These changes in work patterns, values and technology have come together in the trend to freedom. It is now permissible, possible and practical to embrace a life unencumbered by the geographic locales in which our supporting communities and working environments were based, or by restrictive workplaces and practices.

However, we have no control over most of these changes. This does not mean to say we should not understand them. Indeed, the greater our understanding the more we can ensure those freedom drivers do not become slave drivers. Financial life planning and the setting of boundaries play an important role in this new world and can help us make decisions that will affect our lives and money today and for many years to come.

## SOCIETY'S VALUES

At the end of World War II, the overriding value our parents lived by was duty – duty to Queen and country, duty to family, duty to our employers. That's not surprising after a long period of tumultuous conflict. It was a time of austerity. Rationing remained in place until 1954 and National Service until 1960, with the last conscripted servicemen leaving the forces in 1963. However, as we moved into the 60s and 70s, the call of duty began to lessen and a new value began to take its place: freedom. Now we know, from the stories our fathers and grandfathers told us, that freedom is what they were fighting for. I come from a military background. My grandfather, father and both my brothers were career soldiers. I served in the forces in the 1970s, mainly in the British Army on the Rhine. We all served because we believed in freedom. For my grandfather and father freedom meant freedom from tyranny and oppression, a truly noble cause for which they were both wounded and for which many millions died.

For my generation, though, the meaning of freedom began to change. It no longer meant the freedom to pursue a nine to five job working for a single employer, retiring at 65 and then probably dying within 10 years. It meant being able to pursue a life that was more fluid and dynamic. The sexual revolution of the 60s and 70s, the Beatles, the Stones, were all symptomatic of this transition from duty as a core value to freedom.

And then of course Alan Turing, Claude Shannon and Tim Berners-Lee, along with Bill Gates, Steve Jobs and Stephen Wozniak, provided the final catalyst in this transformation; the Internet and the digital world which has produced an IT based society, the route to 'self-expression, choice, individuality – and freedom' as the late Richard Duvall, co-founder of Egg Bank and Zopa, so succinctly put it.

## STEP BY STEP TO CLEAR WATER

**Values:** write down five words that describe your core values. Are they in conflict or harmony with society's values?

## ECONOMY

If there is one thing that characterises Western economies at the moment it is debt. Sovereign debt. Household debt. Corporate debt. All have risen inexorably since the war to the point where debt in some countries approaches or even exceeds the Gross Domestic Product (GDP) of the country.

Debt starts to become a burden and a drag on economic prosperity when the ratio of debt to GDP reaches 85% to 90% of GDP[1]. Above this level, interest and repayment obligations simply kill economic growth, resulting in the horrors of recession such as unemployment and falling wages, both real, physical effects of an economy that does not grow.

Simply put, the 2007/08 financial crisis was a debt-driven, balance-sheet crisis. According to Professors Reinhart and Rogoff[2], authors of a definitive book on the financial crisis written in 2009, the average aftermath of fifteen previous balance-sheet crises was:

> ❯ A 35% fall in real house prices over the following six years
> ❯ A 55% fall in equity prices over the following three and a half years

[1] Cecchetti, Stephen G, Mohanty MS and Zampolli, Fabrizio. *The Real Effects of Debt*, September 2011

[2] Reinhart, Carmen M and Rogoff, Kenneth S. *This time is different; eight centuries of financial folly*, Princetown University Press, 2009

> ‣ Employment falls by 7% over the following four years
> ‣ Output falls by 9% over the following two years
> ‣ Government debt rises by 86% of GDP over the following five years

It's hardly surprising, therefore, that the time for the patient to recover from these financial crises is significantly longer than from other crises. Governments are compelled to cut back and reduce their spend to bring their budgets back into balance. Households realise they are over-extended so take steps to reduce their debt levels by switching income away from spending into debt reduction, then into rebuilding savings. Banks are forced to recapitalise rather than lend money to businesses to use for growth and investment (banks cannot mend and lend at the same time). Even cash-rich businesses prefer to sit on their money rather than invest until they see a recovery in demand for their products.

If that is the bad news, the good news is that if global or regional growth is flat it does not mean that there is no economy or no growth. Some sectors and businesses may be shrinking (and you only have to walk down the high street to see which those are), whilst others are growing successfully through innovation, good marketing and often a successful export strategy. Often these difficult economic times provide amazing opportunities, particularly for forward-thinking small businesses and entrepreneurs.

For some time to come we will be in a low-inflation, low-interest rate environment, which makes financial planning easier, even if it means investment returns are going to stay low for some time.

## INSTITUTIONS AND TRUST

Who do you trust these days? Who do you go to for help and advice? These are important questions that go right to the heart of our establishment and its institutions. Although I believe the majority of our professional advisers and helpers still do an outstanding job, their reputations have been slaughtered by the bad practices of the few. The trust we had in our politicians and local services, our bank manager and the big financial institutions, our financial advisers, solicitors and accountants has all been eroded by scandal, lack of care for the customer, greed and self-interest.

So now you probably rely on the internet to look after your family and friends and source personal networks of friends for advice about what to do, where to go and how to get there. You go online to develop personal and business relationships never before possible. When you want to buy something you no longer go straight to a company website. You probably go first to a forum or discussion group, then talk to your friends (virtual and real) and finally explore the website of a company that other people seem to think works well. Your first port of call for help or advice is often social media, friends, chat rooms, Internet forums, individual reviews on Amazon, TripAdvisor and countless other websites.

The phenomenon even has its own name now – the Zero Moment of Truth. The phrase was coined at Google and, in his book of the same name, Jim Lecinski describes

*'a new decision making moment that takes place a hundred million times a day on mobile phones, laptops and wired devices of all kinds. It's a moment where marketing happens, and where consumers make choices that affect the success and failure of nearly every brand in the world.'*[3]

---

[3] Lecinski, J. *Winning the Zero Moment of Truth*. Google e book available as a free download

Lecinksi seeks to prove his point with some interesting statistics:

- 70% of Americans now say they look at product reviews before making a purchase
- 79% of consumers now say they use a smartphone to help with shopping
- 83% of mothers say they do online research after seeing TV commercials for products that interest them

We have shifted from a vertical decision process to a horizontal decision field, populated by millions offering their own comments and opinions. These individuals might actually be members of the organisation you are researching, or even from the competition. They might be truly genuine people, wanting to help others by describing their experiences. Or they might have a grudge to bear or an idea to peddle. How do you know? Have you ever wondered about that one awful review in a page full of five star reviews? Is it malicious, put there to put you off buying what is actually a perfectly reliable product, or was it a genuine, one-off poor experience?

Does he or she really know what they are talking about, or are they there for sheer self-publicity? This lack of knowledge makes us vulnerable to making the wrong decisions about important issues in our lives. Whether we rely on traditional institutions or a more informal, even anarchic, network of friends, trust is still an issue. Everyone has their own agenda. They want to push their own message. Often they have limited knowledge of the subject under discussion, which can be a dangerous thing.

Trust can be abused, deliberately. In the quarter century to 2008, Bernie Madoff ran a Ponzi scheme from the seventeenth floor of the Lipstick Building in New York. Essentially a vast financial black hole, it sucked in $65 billion of investors' money from around the globe, the majority of which was never seen again. Whilst greed was undoubtedly a factor in this tragedy, trust also played its part. Madoff cultivated an aura of trust by posting consistent, attractive returns that were not excessive. He played the exclusivity card, increasing the demand by keeping prospects at arm's length. He and his acolytes played the social circuits.

In her book on the scandal Erin Arvedlund describes how one follower of Madoff, a Jewish fighter pilot, referred many from his community to Madoff. This individual was *'so highly regarded and so well thought of in his suburban community that many people unquestionably trusted his advice'*[4]. This was a close-knit community of people who had survived the Holocaust and survived the war in the air.

*'They trusted one another with their lives'*. Arvedlund comments that these people were not driven by greed, *'but rather by the desire to invest in their futures with someone they could trust. It was this high level of trust that led smart and savvy people ... to invest with Madoff over the ensuing years without asking serious questions'*.

## STEP BY STEP TO CLEAR WATER

**Trust**: Who you trust, and how much you trust their judgement, is as important an issue today as it was then. Who do you go to for help and advice? What agendas might they have that would bias that advice?

---

[4] Arvedlund, Erin (2009). Madoff: The Man Who Stole $56 Billion (first published as Too Good to be True), Penguin, London

## ENTREPRENEURSHIP AND INFORMATION TECHNOLOGY

Of course, it's not the technology, it's its effect on our personal and working lives that matters. We can all become full participants in the IT based society, the route to *'self-expression, choice, freedom and individuality'*[5]. What is more, the digital networked economy is enabling more and more people to become entrepreneurs.

With our large and growing number of virtual and real connections around the world we are all in a much stronger position to get involved in start-ups and micro-businesses. A characteristic of this type of entrepreneurship is where individuals, their families and other families set up in consumer markets and use word of mouth to spread their ideas, products and services. It is no longer about just designing, producing, buying and selling products and services; it is about becoming part of a new and changing world centred on *'identity, communication, people, markets, brands and trust'* – Richard Duvall and James Alexander again. As our attitude to money changes we and our families are beginning to behave like a small business in which the assets of our homes and income streams blend together.

And the world is becoming more mobile, linked wirelessly. It's both magical and wonderful that you can key (or even speak) 'chemist' or 'bookshop' into your mobile device, and a map comes up with all the nearest stores, with their contact details and information about them and probably a list of customer reviews and ratings.

If you are in manufacturing, you can develop your product virtually, prototype it with a 3-D printer, and outsource the manufacturing to anywhere in the world using websites such as

---

[5] Attributed to Richard Duvall and James Alexander, quoted in Digital Strategy Consulting Thought Leaders paper.

Alibaba, to have a tailor-made product delivered to your door in record time and at a fraction of the cost.

We are all our own publishing houses today. You have an idea. Great. Within a few hours you can convert it into a short e-book and distribute it around the world. As an entrepreneur, you can put together a highly-targeted digital marketing plan that can be implemented over the Internet at a fraction of the cost of print media.

Of course, there is a downside to the mobile digital world. The boundaries between life and work are becoming increasingly blurred. You can, and are often expected to, be contactable by clients or your team anytime, anywhere. You can be in a café, on a train, at a conference and you are still expected to be able to draft up proposals, send e-mails or review presentations – all from your mobile device. Although factories producing physical goods need to be grounded, services can often be provided from a semi- or fully-virtual office. In my own financial planning practice we maintain a small physical office with two staff, and much of the work is carried out by an outsourced team, linked by the Internet and our own virtual office system. And they are not necessarily in the UK; we have had people from as far afield as South Africa and the Philippines working for us through Odesk and People Per Hour.

With today's global phone network, clients can call you, thinking you are in the office, when in fact you are on the slopes. That's fine; you can keep in contact and access their file over Dropbox if that is what life is really about and you are happy to have clients calling you just as you are about to head down the glacier. More importantly, are you really then able and willing to give them your full attention?

"I'll have my secretary do that for you straight away...."

However the revolution in New Entrepreneurship that can provide a perfect balance between life and work is only just starting, as Daniel Priestley points out in his vivid description of the rise of the Global Small Business (GSB).

*'Having a GSB will create an enviable lifestyle. A GSB isn't like having a traditional local small business that prevents the owner from travelling and limits the money they can make to the local economy. The GSB, on the contrary, expands as you travel. For this reason many GSB owners will earn seven-figure salaries with ease.'* [6]

Boundaries are important here, and I will come back to them time and again, especially when we talk about managing time and money. Boundaries are an important tool in helping to develop that life of freedom and independence we seek.

## STEP BY STEP TO CLEAR WATER

**Entrepreneurship**: What does entrepreneurship mean to you? Is it a higher risk strategy that may fail or your route to freedom and independence? Can you think of an opportunity that could be turned into a Global Small Business?

## COMMUNITY AND INFORMATION TECHNOLOGY

Where is your community today, and what does it look like? It used to be at street or village level, or at work. Communities used to be geographically-based, and limited. Technology and transport in days gone by limited travel and communication, so communities grew around the physical – people and places. Communities used to be vertical and hierarchical. Today our communities are global, virtual

---

[6] Priestley, Daniel. *Entrepreneur Revolution*, Capstone, Chichester, 2013

and horizontal. Values and interests now connect communities, not geography or family ties. These global, virtual communities may be vast, such as the American political communities. Conversely, I heard recently of a small group of less than a hundred people with a common interest in fruit stickers. They collect these, and share them over their online community, discuss them and generally have a good, if virtual, time together. Google's social network, Google+, understands this and uses the concept of circles to organise contacts. As Guy Kawasaki puts it in his book *What the Plus*[7], if Facebook is about people, Google+ is about passions and, by extension, communities.

Arguably, location is becoming less important to people as families realise that they can often stay in closer contact through Skype and Facebook than they did when they lived a few miles from each other. Indeed, for you, travel may be becoming a far greater priority, particularly when it is travel with a purpose, a theme we will return to later in this book.

Contacts, content, community – these are the digital drivers of the shifting circles in which we now live and the winds of change are gathering momentum. It's a fabulous opportunity for entrepreneurial families, though with real challenges when it comes to trying to deal with personal finances and achieving life and financial goals. This new world can be the shortcut to freedom; it can also be the Pooh trap that pulls the rug from under you. You cannot control it. You can control things in your own world to take advantage of the winds of change and protect you from the gales.

---

[7] Kawasaki, Guy. *What the Plus*, Mcgraw-Hill, 2012

## LONGEVITY

Diseases that only a few years ago were terminal are now curable. Medical research is doing more than increase our survivability; it is giving many of us healthier, longer and more comfortable lives, although the converse is also true. For many, medicine is simply prolonging a deteriorating quality of life. One of the biggest impacts of medical research and technology advances is increasing longevity, and the impact that will have on our lives, and our children's lives, both socially and financially, is immense.

Here in the UK the results of the most recent population census are starting to come through. According to the Office of National Statistics:

> - At birth, men in the UK can now expect to live, on average, to 79 years, while women will live to 83 years
> - At age 65, the average man in the UK can expect to live a further 18 years while the average woman can expect to live another 21 years
> - At age 85, the average man in the UK can expect to live a further six years while the average woman can expect to live another seven years
> - In 2012 in the UK, 513,000 people were over 90, compared to 385,000 over 90s in 2002

In 1952 the Queen sent less than 3,000 centenary congratulatory telegrams. In 2011 nearly 10,000 centenary cards were sent, along with over 900 105th birthday cards. In 2012 there were 13,350 centenarians in the UK.

Incredibly, a leading British scientist in longevity research, Dr Aubrey de Grey, believes the first person to live to 150 has already been born, whilst others talk about our life spans increasing by a day for every month we live.

"one is sure one is doing more of these than ever!"

The consequence of this increased longevity is simple. We will need more money for when we wind down from work to ensure we outlive our savings. It may also be that we decide to work longer, or live a less-structured life, working fewer days in a year, spending more time doing the things that are important to us. Either way, the concept of building up savings during our working lives in order to fund our later years remains unchanged. What is changing are the figures, both the time and the money.

For our children, longevity is the name of the game. One in three babies born in the UK in 2013 are expected to celebrate their 100th birthday, with boys expected to live for 91 years and girls for 94 years.

## STEP BY STEP TO CLEAR WATER

**Longevity**: How old are you now? Given your health, lifestyle, family history and developments in medicine, how long do you think you will live for? What are the personal and financial implications?

### FAMILY

Probably the most important group in society is the family, and this too has changed and continues to change. The family disintegrated after the war from a coherent, multi-generational unit. It became much less important, with many shunning marriage in favour of long-term partners, high rates of divorce amongst those who had married, and children leaving home and setting up on their own as soon as possible.

Now, though, the pendulum is swinging back, with households under the economic pressures of the global financial crisis reforming as multi-generational units, often based on middle-generation parents housing their own children as well as elderly grandparents.

For the young, life is slowing down. It is taking them longer to find a partner and have children, to find a job or set up their own business, to find their own circle of true friends and indeed their place and role in society.

There is a story about a Catholic priest, an Anglican vicar and a Jewish rabbi discussing when life begins. The priest is adamant that life begins at conception. The vicar argues that it begins at birth. For the rabbi, however, life begins when the kids leave home. If that is so, our rabbi may have a long wait. Children will remain dependent on their parents for far longer, possibly even living with them for much longer because they cannot afford to buy their own homes. Indeed, they are unlikely to own their own home, even with parental support, until well into their 30s.

Today's parents are becoming the central pillars for the multi-generational family. Their own parents are probably just in their 70s, possibly in their late 70s. They may well still be fit and healthy, or they may already be suffering from long-term degenerative diseases such as MS or Alzheimers. Either way, as they bring up their own children, today's parents are also becoming involved in supporting and caring for their parents who may live for many more years whilst growing increasingly frail and infirm.

Parents today have multiple worries about supporting both the upstream and downstream generations (and possibly even the even further downstream generation). They are caught in the middle, so much so that they are known as the Sandwich Generation [8]. The financial implications are profound and the Sandwich Generation will have to become personally well-organised, socially, as parents, and above all financially, to deal with this situation. Managing finances as a multi-generational family unit will become more important than ever to reduce tax and ensure family capital is used efficiently to provide the upstream generation with a good quality of life till death, to help family businesses to flourish and to help the downstream generation get on their feet, become well-educated, and achieve their own independence and freedom sooner rather than later.

---

[8] See www.sandwichgeneration.com

THE SQUEEZED
GENERATION

## LIFE STAGES

Where you are in your life? As you are reading this book, it is reasonable to assume you will have moved through childhood and adolescence, even young adulthood. You are probably now in middle adulthood, possibly married or in a long-term relationship, with children and with a substantial amount of working life ahead of you.

## STEP BY STEP TO CLEAR WATER

**Retirement**: What is your take on retirement? Is it something you look forward to and plan for, or do you intend to keep working until indulging in your own terminal recycling project?

This is the conventional approach to the life cycle. However, according to US financial planner Elizabeth Jetton, you can look at where you are in another way, one which relates to money, although it is not a monetary classification. Once you left school or university, and started to earn some money, you began to get stuff. You entered the accumulation phase of your life, acquiring everything from spouses, children, in-laws (or out-laws), houses, cars, mortgages, furniture, gadgets, any number of personal possessions (and how many of those have now been relegated to the spare room cupboard, the shed or the garage), pets (stick insects, tropical fish – never again please), friends, businesses, photographs, music (all clogging up your hard drive), skis, surf boards and anything else you care to think about.

At your current time of life, however, you are probably over the *getting* phase and more into *doing* things such as bringing up the family, running your own business, competing in competitive or charitable sporting events or participating in any number of creative, cultural and community activities, some of which you may be organising. You could be back at school in one form or another, building knowledge and skills. You will probably be travelling for a restful break or travelling for a purpose such as self-development or to help others. You will be entertaining, and being entertained. You may have a philanthropic agenda that involves active participation in a school or charity as well as donating money. In fact, your diary is so full you will probably be wondering how on earth you will get any time for yourself! Are you even now wondering how much more you can go on doing it, doing it and doing it?

Which is why the next phase of your life will be less about getting or doing and more about *being*. Partly this will be because life's pressures will ease off, enabling you to live more in the moment; partly it will be because you actually have time to look into the future and to recognise that life does not go on for ever. You will start to decumulate; all the stuff that you got will start to go out as its importance fades in the face of your approaching death. A need for personal integrity will grow strongly. You might recognise and foster seeds of spirituality. You may start to take up more contemplative activities such as meditation, walking, gardening. You might try to find the answer to the age-old question 'who am I?' through helping or caring for others, becoming more involved in your community, trying to find out from others their opinion of who you are.

This presents us with a bit of a contradiction. In our early lives we are getting and doing, and spending money in the process. Hopefully we are also saving some money to support us in our later years when we no longer want to spend time and energy earning money. In fact, if you have been super efficient at saving, you could have a significant pot of cash or investments that you don't necessarily want to spend on anything except the basics as you live in the moment and realise that less is more.

---

**Essential personal finance**: This is why financial planning is so important. It enables you to achieve your profound life goals as soon as possible, which is important because we don't know what may happen tomorrow, and it secures your long-term security without leaving a huge surplus of capital, much of which could end up in the hands of the taxman.

---

## YOUR WORLD OF OPPORTUNITY

So this is the environment in which you need to build and develop your personal financial plans, linking them closely with your business plans. Much of this you cannot control. However, it is important you plan those things you *can* control, so you need to be aware of the environment in which you live and work in order to make good decisions.

Those building a life centred on independence, personal integrity and freedom will recognise the higher risks involved; in particular, they will recognise the need to plan and make projections about income and expenditure, and to look at the impact of lifestyle and entrepreneurial decisions on cash flow and wealth.

However, this is also the world of the future in which you want to belong, riding the Freedom Trend. If your integrity has been put under strain in the corporate world a re-assertion of your values, changes in your attitudes to money and work and a highly interconnected world have all come together to give you the opportunity to ride the Freedom Trend.

### POSTSCRIPT

The Freedom Trend has four elements you must get right to ride it successfully. These are **life, time, business** and **money**. It goes without saying that you need to be entrepreneurial in your approach to work, using your passions and skills to build and run your own business in a way that delivers the lifestyle you seek whilst ensuring your customers and team remain committed and supportive.

In this book I address life, time and money in depth, business less so. This book is about creating and implementing a personal life and financial plan, not a business plan. So if you really want to ride the Freedom Trend you also need to look at how to build a business that creates more time, life and money for you. If you are not there already then I recommend you tap into the following:

> **Emyth**. Read Michael Gerber's *Emyth Revisited*. The book is about dealing with the entrepreneurial seizure. Its subtitle is '*Why so many small businesses fail and what to do about it*' and this says it all. Then consider subscribing to emyth.com.

> **Entrevo**. Short for Entrepreneur Revolution, Entrevo was established in Australia and has a presence in Singapore, the UK and the USA. It works closely with Daren Shirlaw and Shirlaws Consulting. Read Daniel Priestley's books *Entrepreneur Revolution* and *Key Person of Influence*, then consider enrolling on the KPI programme.

> **Mike Harris**. Instrumental in founding Egg Bank, First Direct and Mercury Communications, Harris has invaluable insights into starting and building iconic brand businesses. Read *Find Your Light Bulb* and use *The Art of Perfect Pitch* DVDs.

> **Smarta**. Smarta.com provides web-based advice and networking for anyone starting and running a small business.

# Two

# ALL ABOUT PLANNING

'Someone's sitting in the shade today because someone
planted a tree a long time ago.'

WARREN BUFFET

This book is about personal life and financial planning, so the underlying assumption I have made is that planning is 'A Good Thing.' Any entrepreneurial business owner would accept this. After all, a key ingredient for business success is planning so it is surprising how many people think planning their lives and personal finances is absolutely not necessary. In spite of Benjamin Franklin's advice that '*by failing to prepare, you are preparing to fail*', many people seem to have such confidence in their ability to make and retain significant fortunes that personal financial planning is seen as unnecessary, even spineless.

To plan, or not to plan, that is the question, and I believe there are sound reasons why the entrepreneurial family should plan their lives and personal finances, as well as their businesses, not least to co-ordinate personal and business objectives and finances. You might argue that you should separate your business from your personal life. Families after all don't really want work brought back home. However you, the independent entrepreneurial business owner, wear two hats, the other as a member of a family, and an important member at that. You are probably the person responsible in the main (though not entirely) for putting food on the table, and you are also a loving and supportive parent to your children. Two hats, one person; you cannot entirely separate your roles. You will have to align your business and personal goals, your business and personal finances, your business and personal life. You cannot work with just one hat. To be successful (by which I mean happy, carefree, part of a loving relationship, living life that achieves profoundly important goals for you) you have to expect to wear both hats, bringing them into alignment.

You are probably already idealistic in your approach to business. A 2014 research study by Oxford University found that 73% of 2,000 young professionals surveyed ranked social contribution above profits as a personal career goal. In fact, you are probably in the business you are in because it *does* reflect your values and ideals.

I established my own businesses because I was angry at the way financial services treated the consumer, as well as consumers' general lack of understanding of money that led many into serious difficulties. Indeed, many clients come to me because they have over-extended into property, taken on too much debt and find themselves asset rich, cash poor. I wanted to change the way people think about and deal with money. I wanted them to get back to using money as a tool, not as an end in itself.

Look at Jane Ni Dhulchaointigh who has set up her own company to manufacture and sell her own invention – Sugru, dubbed the best invention since Sellotape. Sugru is silicone putty that you can mould into any shape before it sets, so it can be used to repair things, or to adapt things that don't do quite what we want them to. The important thing is that Jane has done it because she is passionate about tearing down the throwaway society. She wants the world to learn to adapt and mend objects rather than throwing them away, and is giving them the means to do so.

## STEP BY STEP TO CLEAR WATER

**Passion:** What are you passionate about in your business or work? What drives you to do what you do or would like to do? How do you plan to change the world?

Jane, you and I are probably all in the game of changing the world for the better. Changing the world does not happen by chance; it comes through careful research and planning. That includes personal life and financial planning as well as business planning. No plan, no change.

### PLANNING PRODUCES RESULTS

I am passionate about planning because I know that, in general, it leads to success, although its inevitability can take the edge off life. I recall my first sales job in financial services, many years ago, cold calling to make appointments to sell insurance. I had an excellent manager who, unusually in financial services in those days, made me plan my target market, pitch, call strategy, everything. And just about the first call I made was spot on, leading to an appointment made in less than two minutes. I, my manager, my colleagues knew it was going to work. And it did.

In 2012 I was determined to achieve a time in the Great North Run half marathon of under two hours and fifteen minutes, so I planned a training programme and developed a plan for race day that worked perfectly. I crossed the finish line in two hours thirteen minutes, as I knew I would do before I had even crossed the start line.

Even these small examples show that planning works. The principle applies all the time, whether I am running a client workshop, taking the family on holiday, providing a new service for clients, even writing this book, planning produces results. If there is one downside it is that planning leads to that inevitability in life. You don't get quite the same thrill from achieving something having planned rather than winged it.

Some will argue that planning leaves no room for spontaneity, that important act of grasping the moment and running with it, going for what the world sends in our direction rather than trying to direct the world to our own ends all the time. Paradoxically, a well-planned life and finances can allow you to be more spontaneous. With the confidence of knowing where you are and where you are going, it is often easier to be more spontaneous (especially if it comes to spending money) than if you don't know where you are or where you are going.

And indeed we can over-plan, sometimes with disastrous results. History in particular provides catastrophic examples of planning failures. Take the Battle of the Somme in the summer of 1916; Haig's immensely detailed battle plan ran to 57 pages of orders, logistics and timetables that he thought left nothing to chance. Based on a completely erroneous appreciation of the battle situation and with no flexibility, the plan led to four months of bitter fighting, 600,000 dead and wounded and a British advance of just six miles, not the brief battle and the definitive breakthrough that Haig had expected.

## PLAN IT OR WING IT?

Indeed, the fact that plans rarely survive contact with reality is often cited as a pivotal argument for not planning. So what are the alternatives? Well, you wing it, you take life as it comes, you act on your instincts and impulses. With a good deal of chutzpah, a hefty dose of confidence, a wing and a prayer and a bit of *carpe diem* you might well achieve great things, and get a real thrill and sense of achievement when you do.

## STEP BY STEP TO CLEAR WATER

**Planning:** Set down examples in your life of planned and unplanned successes and failures. What are the lessons you can take away from these stories? Are you a planner or a winger?

ICARAUS Snr        ICARUS

I believe in the importance of living in the moment. The present is where we can really *be*. Financial life planning will actually help you to be really present in the moment because it removes the worry and fear of the future and stops you having to constantly think about where you are going next. As importantly, the 'wing it' approach leaves the balance between the present and the future too much in favour of the present and takes little account of the future.

So what are we planning for in our financial life plan? In my view, four things:

1. To develop a practical framework for running household finances
2. To achieve profound life and financial goals as fast as possible
3. To ensure long-term financial security
4. To deal with life's setbacks

**Essential personal finance**: Planning creates the balance between living in the moment (because we don't know what is going to happen tomorrow) and taking responsibility for the longer term (because many tomorrows may remain). If we achieve these four elements the result should be nothing less than freedom.

## Financial framework

Many people today lack a financial framework or system. They are overwhelmed by piles of papers and policy documents, derived from policies and investments purchased haphazardly over the years with no overall plan. When asked where a product fits into the scheme of things answers range from 'It looked good in the weekend money section advertisement' to 'My brother-in-law recommended it.'

When it comes to expenses, the core of financial planning, we often enter a fantasy world. To be fair, some families can give a reasonable estimate of their living expenses. Others have no idea and, worst of all, some think they know what they spend each month or year, only later to discover they have been badly off target, usually on the downside.

> **Essential personal finance:** current and future expenditure is the key to successful financial planning. We need to organise our money to enable us to achieve our spending plans, and our spending plans should derive from our deepest life goals. Financial planning is about having the right money in the right place at the right time to achieve our goals.

Even families who have a reasonably accurate set of current financial statements (assets, liabilities, income, expenditure and estate) are rarely able to project what those statements look like ten or even five years in the future. Usually families have little idea what their income will be when they wind down or stop working.

Without labouring the point, my own experience is that many families live in a state of ongoing financial disorganisation. Indeed, one of the key reasons they decide to visit a financial planner in the first place is to achieve clarity about their financial situation, both now and in the future. These are some of the things my clients tell me when I ask them for the reason for their first visit:

- 'We are not fully in control of our finances'
- 'We feel we are on the cusp of making a serious wrong decision'
- 'We are looking for a way to create a longer term view of our finances, to give us room to live and breathe, to give us more choice and freedom'
- 'I don't understand money; all I feel around money is fear and anxiety'
- 'We are working hard for our money, but we are not sure our money is working hard for us'
- 'I have limited skills and knowledge around money'

> ‘We don’t know where we are now or where we will be in the future’
> ‘We seem unable to live the lifestyle we aspire to’

When families do achieve clarity it usually provides a huge sense of relief, even if the picture does not look good. At least they now know where they stand, and can take appropriate action.

### STEP BY STEP TO CLEAR WATER

**Financial statements:** Describe your feelings if you were asked to prepare statements of your assets, liabilities, income and expenditure in the next 30 minutes. What do your feelings tell you?

## Goals

We live in an era where money is made for its own sake, not as the fuel to live a fulfilled life that it should be. Often finances are managed not to support a particular lifestyle or value; instead, using money to make more money seems to be the fashion. Money is a proxy for the ego, and financial decisions are often made to protect or massage our egos, not to support the achievement of our deepest life goals.

Life and money are deeply intertwined. I would suggest that you cannot make profound changes to your life without making serious money decisions to support your plans, both at the human level and the numbers level. Similarly, you cannot make good financial decisions without having a very clear idea of your life projects and lifestyle. These will translate into financial objectives at some point, and are derived from your expectations of what you want to achieve, the values by which you want to live your life, not a random figure or date plucked out of the sky.

Goals provide direction, confidence and energy. With a clear vision, you can set out the steps to get you there and deal with the hurdles and fastballs that will try to thwart you. Your personal projects, lifestyle aspirations, values, needs and drives all provide the *raison d'être* for your financial plan and its decisions. Have you in the past brought a financial product, and within a few years stopped paying the premiums, let it lapse or even cashed it in, even though you were told at the point of sale that this is a product for the long term? The answer is almost certainly yes, if the life policy lapse rate in the UK in the past was anything to go by. And why did you let it lapse? Probably because it lacked any relevance to your life (or at least that was your perception).

**Essential personal finance**: the sequence to follow is goals, plan, products.

I am occasionally asked to comment on an investment someone has read about or that a friend has told them about. They want to know if they should invest in the product (everyone says it will do really well, there seems to be no downside, etc). I always answer the question with another question: *'Will investing in this product enable you to achieve your goals more quickly and efficiently? How does this product support your plan to achieve your goals?'* More often than not, when they think it through, the answer is that it doesn't.

**Essential personal finance**: the primary criterion for buying a financial product or service (or any product or service for that matter) is whether it supports or hinders the achievement of your life goals

**Long-term security**

I have talked about the impact of increasing longevity on family finances. This is something that has to be addressed, and the earlier the better. The keys to dealing with this are the Three Drivers of Financial Freedom: savings, compound interest and asset allocation, which I cover in detail in Chapter Seven. However saving implies a reduction in spending, and potentially the hijacking of those important and immediate life goals. Financial life planning will help to resolve these conflicts between the short and long term.

What you are really going to achieve from well-formulated goals and a structured, considered life and financial plan can be expressed in one word – freedom.

**Dealing with the unexpected**

You need to be able to deal with the unexpected. Life will have kicked you in the teeth in the past, and sure as eggs are eggs, it will do so again in the future. Accept it, and plan for it. Life can throw a huge range of fast balls at us, from the irritating and not too serious car breakdown or mild storm damage to serious injury or illness or even the death of a close family member. Put in place some contingency plans centred around a Security Fund and insurance. No one likes insurance: it is usually seen as money down the drain, though I have yet to meet a widow who complained her husband was over-insured.

**FREEDOM**

Freedom is a central theme of this book, so what exactly is freedom? It is certainly not the right to behave in society irrespective of the rights and happiness of others and it is more than being confined to your own world because of a lack of understanding of where you are and where you are going. Often that lack of understanding relates to money, a source of anxiety, even pain. It is fear of money, amongst other things, that confines us.

**Essential personal finance:** Freedom comes from defining and setting boundaries and living a life dedicated to achieving your goals within those boundaries. Greater freedom comes from personal growth, the means by which we can expand our boundaries.

Lianne's wonderful story is a fabulous illustration of the power of boundaries. Lianne, a mother of two, had gone through a very difficult divorce. She was left to bring up the children whilst working in the public sector for a very modest salary. When she first came to me for help I asked her about her spending habits. She admitted to being a compulsive spender, especially when life really got her down. Her cupboards were full of clothes and shoes, purchased to make her feel better, though hardly worn. Her larder was full because she never planned her shopping and often ended up buying unnecessary extra food.

However, she was clear she wanted to love, support and educate her children. She wanted to be a really good mother to them to make up for the disaster of the marriage. She wanted to ensure her children were able to work hard for their exams, as well as having a happy childhood. Both she and her children loved music and wanted to go to concerts. Lianne, when she first came to see me, ruled this out because she *did not have any money*.

I worked with her to plan her boundaries. We started on her life goals, refining them and adding detail. Next, we tackled her spending. I asked her to start recording and categorising all her spending, which she did with those simplest of tools, a notebook and pencil, which she carried with her always (and still does). Each week she totted up the figures and as time went on a clear picture of her spending emerged. Next, we went back to her goals, and using her spending history and her costed-out goals we developed an annual spending plan which, not surprisingly, cut down on unnecessary clothing and food, and included a sum for fun with her children, concerts in particular.

I recall one Monday morning after we had been working together for a while. She called me to talk about her weekend. She had taken the girls to London to see their favourite group in concert. She and the children had had a fabulous time. What really made the whole story so heartening was that she had done it all without any feelings of guilt or anxiety over money. It had been in her plan. She knew she could spend the money without compromising her other necessary expenditures. She had achieved her goal of bringing happiness and fun to her children in a way that left them all feeling over the moon.

This was all about boundaries. She had set herself boundaries (and quite narrow ones at that), and within those boundaries she had achieved real freedom, the freedom to meet a particular goal, to be free of pain and anxiety, to be there in the moment with her children, simply to be. That is what freedom is all about.

## STEP BY STEP TO CLEAR WATER

**Boundaries:** look at your own life and write down an example of a self-imposed boundary. What is its effect on your life and the lives of your partner or family? Think of a situation where you lack control and setting boundaries would help.

## IT'S THE PROCESS THAT MATTERS

Plans rarely survive contact with reality, to misquote Moltke. I think there is a certain truth in this, although I have met families who put plans together over 10 years ago, plans that have stood them in good stead throughout that time with very little change needed to enable them to live the life they really want to live. However, reality for many of us will cause a change of direction, maybe even an entire rewrite, especially as we come up against the obstacles to our plans.

I would, therefore, emphasis that it is as much about the process of planning as the plan itself and whether you go through it yourself or are taken through it by a financial coach or planner it will be enormously beneficial.

The Financial Planning Standards Board, the international organisation that oversees financial planners who carry the Certified Financial Planning licence requires planners to use a six-stage process for developing a financial plan. The Kinder Institute of Life Planning advocates a five-step process called EVOKE to develop a life plan. In my own practice I have incorporated both methodologies into a six-stage process for drawing up a financial life plan called FUTURE:

> - **Foundation**: a full inventory and analysis of your life and finances forms the foundation of the plan, including assumptions and an analysis of your risk profile
> - **Utopia**: establishing what you want to have, to do, to be; a profound exploration of your goals
> - **Transformation**: identifying and dealing with the obstructions on the road to utopia
> - **Utilisation of resources**: establishing the best option for your existing resources, both personal and financial, including life time cash flow planning

> **Roadmap**: creating the plan to get you from where you are now to where you want to be
> **Execution**: implementing and living the plan

In my practice, a Mapmaker meeting precedes this planning process. This is to establish the client's financial planning needs and suitability, and to discuss the most appropriate route for the client to move forward.

More importantly, having developed a plan with the client, we work with them on an annual cycle to coach, guide, encourage, advise and, if necessary, provide a kick in the pants to them to implement their plan. The starting point for each annual cycle is a renewal of the plan to take into account any changes in the previous 12 months.

## THE FRUITS OF THE PROCESS

We all in the financial community trust our processes, because we know they bring results, results that are more than just a written plan.

You will develop a personal inventory, including property, goods and chattels, family, friends, businesses and business partners.

Then you will put together an inventory of your life. This will include a detailed set of accurate financial statements comprising a schedule of assets, liabilities, income and expenditure. You will also have an estate statement, setting out what happens in the event of your or your partner's death. By the end of the process you should have all the facts at your disposal to enable you to make an informed decision about your money.

Self-understanding builds on this base and by the time you are well into the process you should be able to articulate your deepest and most profound goals and the values that you want to live by. In doing so, you will find yourself energised, focused and far sighted. As Stephen Covey, author of *The Seven Habits of Highly Effective People*, put it, begin with the end in mind.

The importance of this principle was brought home to me on my first driving lesson. My instructor asked me to drive along a winding country road between Ampleforth and Oswaldkirk in North Yorkshire. Frankly, I was all over the place and after a few hundred yards my instructor wrenched on the handbrake before we plummeted over the edge. He asked me where I was looking. I told him that, of course, I was looking at the road directly in front of the car. He patiently suggested instead I look as far ahead as possible after which I kept a straight course along the line of the road. The point was well made, and well taken.

You will be able to develop and assess options, make informed decisions about your life and money, set down a plan and execute it.

Finally, you will learn about money. If you are working with a coach or adviser you will have a raft of financial principles and products explained to you. If you are on this route on your own you will need to educate yourself, and there are plenty of resources out there to help.

## POSTSCRIPT

What does planning mean to you now? Does it appeal, or are you still going to wing it? Or do I hear you say 'Yes, but...' (If you have read the book carefully so far you will note I have not used the word 'but' except in someone else's quote, nor will I do so). Possibly you have been meaning to do this for months, if not years. Starting something is always the most difficult step, especially if you don't know where you are going.

'If you don't know where you are going,
you'll end up someplace else'

YOGI BERRA

Take some time to think deeply about planning your money and your life. If you are already doing it ask if it is bringing results, and if not, why not. If you aren't, set out the list of 'buts', discuss them with your spouse, partner and family as appropriate. Then (and here is the difficult part) make a commitment to developing and implementing your own financial life plan within a realistic time frame. The rest of this book will provide you with more than adequate help and guidance.

# Three

## CLEAR THE DECKS

'Give me six hours to chop down a tree and I
will spend the first four sharpening the axe.'

ABRAHAM LINCOLN

'Spectacular achievement is always preceded
by unspectacular preparation.'

ROBERT H SCHULLER

Planning your life and money is probably the most important
activity you will undertake, since its result is happiness and
freedom, goals achieved, great family and relationships, a truly
fulfilled life. Ergo, you need to create time and space for this most
important activity. This is more than just preparation; this is the
important first step in the planning process.

The ancient Greeks had a word for it: *kenosis*, an emptying of
oneself. Karen Armstrong, albeit in a slightly more spiritual context,
describes this as an *'emptying of yourself of the greed, selfishness and
preoccupation that, perhaps inevitably, are engrained in our thoughts
and behaviours but are also the source of much of our pain'*[9].

Armstrong goes on to say that *'once you give up the nervous
craving to promote yourself, denigrate others, draw attention to your*

---

[9] Armstrong, Karen, *The Case for God*, Vintage 2009, p29

*unique and special qualities and ensure you are the first in the pecking order, you experience an immense peace'*. It is this inner peace that provides the emotional space to develop a good plan.

What we are really trying to do here is to bring our egos under control, particularly in relation to money. Money and the ego are entwined. Money is often a proxy for the ego; it can, of course, also be a threat. We use money in so many ways to let our ego express itself, often to the detriment of our true selves and what we really want to be and do. Similarly, money issues can also leave the ego threatened and vulnerable, leading to bad financial decisions.

What is the ego's role in our lives? Primarily it is our protector, if you will, deriving from what Conrad Lorenz described as the Parliament of Instincts or the Four Fs: fight, flight, food and reproduction. These are the driving forces behind our survival and the survival of the species and they lead, if not checked, to an entirely self-centred, compassionless life in which we remain trapped in our own instinctual environment without room to develop and grow. If we make any impact on the world, it is likely to be bad.

So, letting go of the ego and its instinctual pressures is a prerequisite for a profound, outward-looking life plan. It also means leaving our comfort zone and taking risks. We often protect our ego with ideas, messages, thoughts that we cling to, even if they are ultimately damaging, because we are at home with them. Clinging to the familiar, especially if it is one with less than positive outcomes, leads us nowhere.

## CLINGING AND LETTING GO

If we let these falsehoods go we can spread our wings and truly grow. The greatest freedom we can ever enjoy involves staying true to ourselves and ignoring the hype and lies that surround us.

Clinging on to possessions and beliefs from the past will make sure that freedom always eludes us. This idea of complete freedom was espoused in a more mythical and spiritual age than ours. The *Tao Te Ching*, the sacred text of Taoism, recommends that you '*Empty your mind of all thoughts. Let your heart be at peace.*'

The empty mind is able to receive new ideas, messages and directions. We need to clear our lives of the detritus that is so apparent in our offices, homes and minds. By doing so, we can open ourselves up to a revolutionary way of looking after our finances, one that can change our lives in a remarkable way. Many people are afraid to try new things in the belief that failure is the biggest defeat. However, the inability to even countenance new ideas is more damaging.

Can you see where we are heading with this? There is, probably, deep down within you, some dream or goal you really want to achieve. Whilst it is wrapped up in your ego's protective warmth, unable to escape, it will never be achievable. Letting go of your comfort blanket and protector brings peace and internal freedom. It creates space for your ideas and dreams to take wing. And once you let them grow and develop, they won't fade away. On the contrary, they will energise you, give you courage to escape your comfort zone, lead you into the sun-filled uplands of a deeply fulfilled life.

The 2009 Disney Pixar film *Up*, which you might well have seen with your children, provides a wonderful example of this. Our hero Carl is forced by circumstances throughout the film to let go of the physical and emotional burdens he has carried since the death of his beloved wife, Ellie. In one scene, Carl throws all the furniture out of his house, including his favourite chair. Although he does this of necessity, the result is spectacular. He physically takes off and he sloughs off many of his cares and sorrows. He finds his new purpose. He becomes energised, inspired, even youthful.

At the end Carl gives Russell, his young fellow traveller, the Ellie Badge he has worn since childhood. It is a generous and graceful act that honours Ellie, releases Carl from all his burdens and empowers Russell.

## STEP BY STEP TO CLEAR WATER

**Letting go:** Watch *Up.*

Letting go can feel like a euphemism for belt tightening or budgeting. However, letting go is not the fashion statement of the Age of Austerity. It is a long-standing philosophy that will change your life in a spiritual, emotional and physical way. The 18th-century English mystic poet William Blake beautifully expressed how letting go was the gateway to true freedom in his poem 'Eternity':

> *'He who binds to himself a joy*
> *Does the winged life destroy;*
> *But he who kisses the joy as it flies*
> *Lives in eternity's sunrise.'*

Blake's words resonate as clearly now as they did when written two centuries ago.

**Essential personal finance:** Planning is designed to help you fulfil your goals and dreams and the first step is to learn how to let go of things that hold you back.

## SAYING 'NO'

Letting go in a practical sense is important. We live in a busy world, as you have probably noticed. More than that, 'busyness' seems to create 'busyness'. You are probably busy because you are good at what you do, creating further demand for your products or services.

> 'If you want something doing,
> give it to a busy person'.

### STEP BY STEP TO CLEAR WATER

**Busyness**: think about how often you are asked to do things by other people, both in business and in your personal life, which detract from your time and distract you from your real life goals.

Saying 'no' is a simple and effective way of getting more time for oneself, and letting go of an overly cluttered life. What should be the criteria when responding to a request for help from someone else? The short answer is your own life goals. Maybe a request fulfils a goal; for instance, a request to help in the local arts centre could meet your objective of becoming more involved in the community. At other times a request may not fit in with your own life goals and actually has the potential to distract you. And so having our own goals and values sorted out helps you to provide you with criteria for when to say 'no'.

"I'm Practising saying 'No' and quite good at it by the look of things!"

This may seem a self-centred approach to life, unless of course your goals and values are compassionate and humanitarian and work to your strengths, which will almost certainly be the case as we will see in the next chapter. In some ways in business it is much easier because you will have defined business goals to provide clarity about what you should or should not be doing.

Charity is another area in which saying no is often difficult. If we agreed to every request we receive for charity we would never have any time for ourselves, and little cash left. Saying 'no' can often lead to intense feelings of guilt and shame. This is where having a charitable plan works well.

## STEP BY STEP TO CLEAR WATER

**Charity**: spend some time thinking through what causes you want to be involved with. Identify organisations working in that area, select one or two for your attention and stick with them.

When next asked by a charity not on your list you can say 'no' without shame or guilt and tell them why. In my own case I want to give the young a chance. I also have an interest in education, and find the hunger we see in less developed parts of the world obscene against the backdrop of our own affluence. For me Mary's Meals fits the bill. The organisation works in schools in lesser-developed parts of the world, where they build kitchens on the school site and train parents to cook a square meal for each student who comes to school every day. This encourages pupils to come to school and prevents hunger getting in the way of learning. I support it and am able to say 'no' to other charitable requests with ease.

It goes without saying that saying 'no' without care can damage or demean. There is an art to saying 'no' gracefully and with compassion by reflecting back to the person so that they are not belittled. Indeed, a conversation can show how the task could be done differently, faster, or by someone else other than you. Often we can guide the person to rethink their request in a constructive way that helps them to develop personally and see things in a new way.

The other side of the coin is that many people who desperately need help will not ask for it out pride, fear of rejection or a lack of self-worth. In such situations, it may be that it is in everyone's interest for us to volunteer our assistance. Once again, whether you do that will depend your values and goals.

## THE INTERNET

The Internet has an insidious effect on our time. A search for some information, which you may think will only take a few minutes, might well turn into an hour-long trawl, without any perceptible result or benefit. Hours can be spent on Facebook, Twitter, LinkedIn and the hundreds of other social media sites. E-mails pour in from around the world, solicited or not.

Use of the Internet needs to be controlled, boundaries and criteria set, time limited. Facebook serves my goal of maintaining contact with my circle of friends and my various communities, enabling me to apply the principles of quality, not quantity, and less is more to my Facebook interactions. My control boundaries in this case are set by value rather than time or money.

---

### STEP BY STEP TO CLEAR WATER

**The Internet:** Tomorrow, log the time you spend sharing thoughts, words, photos, music, ideas. Are you surprised at the figure? Does this time on the net actually further the achievement of your goals?

## POSSESSIONS

Have a look round your house. As one who has probably spent much of the last 20 years in the accumulation or *getting* phase of your life, you may find it a little cluttered. The garage, the spare room and the attic are particular suspects, where piles of junk lie unused, uncared for. Does it prey on your mind? All those nick-nacks and gadgets that need maintaining, repairing, cleaning, are they really necessary?

You have probably moved from *getting* to *doing* if you are reading this book, and in time will move to the *being* phase of your life, and from there to the ultimate letting go experience of your death. Why wait to then to deal with your stuff (by which time you will be beyond being able to deal with it anyway)? Consider accelerating the process a little (or a lot). Someone, somewhere can make use of the stuff you have not used for years. It may have a value, and you can sell it on Ebay or at a car boot sale (preferably without buying something else to take home). You might want to donate it to charity.

I mentioned Mary's Meals above. The charity also runs the Backpack Project to provide from voluntary donations a school bag and a range of clothing and equipment for children in the schools.

When my family and I first did this we were amazed at the result. We found a number of my son's old school bags and I had a pile of unused conference bags. We found clothes, pens, pencils, toys – virtually everything requested by the organisers – by going through all our cupboards and drawers and then those of our friends. We filled seven bags, lightened the loads in our house and minds, and provided a magnificent present to seven children at a school in Africa.

You won't want to get rid of everything, of course, and your home will fill up with stuff, as ours has. My wife and I occasionally look back to the day we completed on our house. For various reasons we were unable to move in straight away, so that evening we had a few friends round for an upstanding celebratory drink in an empty house. We always think the house, empty of possessions and filled with the laughter and conversation of good friends, was at its best that day.

## BRINGING YOUR BUSINESS HOME

There are other practices and procedures you could consider to help you in this process of emptying, letting go. Some of these will be used in your business and can be adapted to the home. I have already mentioned the value of setting boundaries, and in common with this you should set priorities. Unsurprisingly, these will often become clearer as your deepest and most profound goals, the values by which you want to lead your life, become clearer (as they will, I promise you). Priorities enable us to quickly make informed choices, spending less time on the decision, and making the decision with confidence.

As a business owner you will undoubtedly rely on a range of systems and processes. If these work well they should leave you with more time for strategic thought, and planning. They should also provide you with a peace of mind, knowing your team is doing it for you, correctly and well. That on its own should be a weight off your mind, allowing you time and emotional space for clear thought about you and your family. I will never forget a speech I heard from Michael Gerber, author of *The E-myth*. He asked us what our most important role was as business owners. Of course we all gave the answers you would expect: marketing, finance, operations, strategy etc. Gerber's answer to his own question was a revelation. He said *'Your primary role as a business owner is to create more life for yourself'*. Wow, and isn't that just right? And for Gerber, the lynchpin for achieving this is systems and processes, delegated out to your teams.

In a less formal way, you can use systems and processes in your own home. At its simplest, this might be having a system for putting your car keys in the same place every time you come home – which at least avoids the stress and trauma of having to find them the next morning. You could have a tick box system for the end-of-the-month things that need doing, a simple sheet of paper you can photocopy which lists all those mundane tasks someone has to do. Dishwasher salt check, fill car wash bottles, pay the paper bill, check smoke alarm batteries – the list goes on. The list does two things; it helps you ensure you get the important things done, reducing worry and stress. And you let go of a burden that will hold you back from achieving the important things.

## STEP BY STEP TO CLEAR WATER

**Checklist:** identify an aspect of home life that causes frustration and anxiety. Try breaking it down into a checklist which you copy and use each time the event occurs.

### CHILL OUT!

Go away! Once a year, take a long weekend with your spouse and partner. Leave the children, the cat and the dog, your elderly parents, the tropical fish in someone else's care, and go off somewhere. Let go of your life, family, home for a couple of days, and take time to review your life, your goals and your values, your money. Be generous and forgiving to yourselves and think about the forthcoming year, what it will hold for you, what you want to achieve and how you are going to do it.

Finally, when you are so busy, when the world is pounding at your door, screaming for your time and demanding your product or service, when you don't seem to have any time for anything – then take time out to meditate, a practice I address in Chapter 10.

### WHAT COMES OUT OF LETTING GO?

Well, you are on the road to asceticism, the counterculture to materialism. You will have cleared the decks, physically, emotionally and spiritually. You will have created for yourself a clean sheet of paper on which you can start to build a truly amazing financial life plan. You will already be on the road to a more fulfilled, less stressed life and you should be feeling a sense of calm and confidence. You will be grounded in reality, having given up listening to the opinions of others, opinions that may not be worth the air they are spoken with, and you will be well able to listen to what your own heart and mind is telling you. All in all you are now set to begin the process of planning your life and money for a life of freedom, and that starts, in the next chapter, with a voyage of self-discovery and the creation of your personal and family inventory.

## POSTSCRIPT

Take the first step – which is often the most difficult. Start with a simple exercise around possessions. Find a drawer, box or cupboard, one that is out of the way, ignored and which you know to be full of stuff not looked at for years. Aim to empty it by making a decision about every object. Decide to use it (so put it somewhere accessible and useable), recycle it, give it away, sell it or dispose of it. If it is paper (such as a letter, press clipping, programme) consider scanning it. At least it will be easily accessible on your computer to read from time to time.

If you cannot deal with it immediately (you may have to wait for a suitable car boot sale), make a commitment to a specific event and go to it.

# Four

# SELF-DISCOVERY

'Knowing yourself is
the beginning of all wisdom.'

ARISTOTLE

'Who in the world am I?
Ah, that's the great puzzle.'

LEWIS CARROLL, *ALICE IN WONDERLAND*

A plan is like a building. If it is going to stay upright it needs firm foundations, and the greater the detail the more enduring the result. I remember once asking a top London architect if he got bored doing all that detail work (this was in the days before computer generated boxes). He looked at me with a glint in his eye and said, *'The detail is the building'*.

So it is with financial life planning: you have to create a good foundation on which to build your plan. This is the inventory of your life and your family (and your business, to a certain extent). The more detailed you make this, the better.

This inventory, by the way, is not just about money and figures. It is really about you and your family, all unique and individual human beings. It is about your thoughts and feelings, your goals and values, your friends, your *stuff*. You will be asking yourself a lot of 'what' questions: 'what do I own, what do I have?' Then you will think about what you do each day, each month at work and at home.

And of course you will address those great, possibly unanswerable questions: 'who am I?' and 'what do I really want to be?'

You might also start to ask yourself some 'Why?' questions. Why did I do this? Why did I buy that? Why did I stop doing that? You probably want to avoid doing too much of this. We are looking at the future, and what is now, is. There is little point in looking back, and in particular there is no point in fretting over past errors, regretting things you did or did not do, except to learn lessons that might be worth noting (and indeed to take an appreciative, enquiring approach to your life, looking back on when you were at your best, when things were going really well, is a useful exercise). However, this is an exercise in setting a starting point – the here and now – and moving forward.

## STEP BY STEP TO CLEAR WATER

**Time:** Write down what time it is in your life on a 24-hour clock? What does that mean to you?

### RECORDING

Before you start, find some means of recording your thoughts, feelings, ideas, facts, conversations, some way to note down those fleeting ideas, things you remember when you wake in the darkest hour before dawn. In our technology-driven world, I recommend an old-fashioned notebook and pencil, such as a Moleskine, something smart, tough and worthy of these important thoughts and facts. This is *'My Life Book'*. Computers tend to be distracting and less accessible than paper and pencil. Light bulb moments need instant attention.

Having said that, your computer or smartphone will of course have a role to play. You are bound to need a spreadsheet at some point. You might want to record some of your thoughts in audio form, either to save in that form, for instant conversion to type, or for transcription at a later date.

Applications like Day One or iReminisce can also be very useful. Day One provides a little icon in the menu bar of your Mac and clicking it instantly opens a window into which you can write without having to open the application itself. And it is stored securely in the cloud for easy retrieval later.

## RELATIONSHIPS

Your own close circle is a good place to start.

### STEP BY STEP TO CLEAR WATER

**Relationships:** take a piece of A3 paper (or even A2, or a flipchart page) and some coloured pens, and draw a family tree or mind map, taking it out as far as you feel your sphere of influence takes you.

As you draw each line, add bits of detail such as ages and health issues. Grade relationships by importance, identify possible challenges in the family that are already there or might arise in the future. Think about where your resources might need to be directed today and in the future. This exercise will help you discover the real meaning of Sandwich Generation.

Look at relationships in terms of both immediacy and importance. Identify immediate issues that need to be addressed today. You might, in some cases, want to make the connecting line between you and an individual a bit thicker, or use a traffic light system of red, amber and green to categorise the relationship.

For instance, if your son or daughter, in the sixth form, is having difficulty at school and not making good progress it is both immediate and urgent and warrants a thick red line.

You will find an interesting infographic appears that helps you see your family circle in a new light, one which shows where resources are going to be needed, where the priorities are. Of course, the fact that your eldest child, well organised, with it, keen, is coloured green, connected with a thin line, does not mean he is ignorable. Far from it; he needs your time and love and your family tree will help to allocate appropriate resources for him.

You might at this stage want to get out your address book and take an inventory of your friendships, maybe note down old friends not seen for a while, or ever-present people you might wish were not actually around so much. Who are those five friends who are absolutely important to you, above all others, who will support you in time of crisis, and who you would drop everything for if they were in trouble? Think about what you want to do with them. When did you last contact them? Why are they so important? Are they still important, or have both you and they moved on, leaving the relationship a relic and fond memory of the past, one that can now be gently released?

## STEP BY STEP TO CLEAR WATER

**Friends**: you are never too old to make new friends. Who have you bumped into recently whom you think could become really important in your life? Think about whether you should be pursuing and developing that relationship.

MMMMMMM
er

I'm trying to think of five friends

## STRENGTHS AND OPPORTUNITIES

Now move back to you – and your strengths. Self-assessment can
be difficult and there are many tools to help you carry out a good,
objective self-assessment. Consider taking a psychometric or
personality test (in fact, you probably have already done so) such
as the Kolbe Test, which gives you an indication of how you

instinctively act in a situation, enabling you to focus on instinctive modes of action you do well, or Myers Briggs, based on Jung's theory of personality types and the interactions between them.

A less well-known and useful test is the Strengthfinder Test. You need to buy the book with the answers in it, and it is more subjective than the psychometric tests, giving a range of possible areas in which you are strong.

I am really grateful to two of my American friends from the financial planning community, Phil Dyer of Dyer Financial Advisory and Lisa Kirchenbauer of Omega Wealth Management (who together run a consultancy called Total Business Transformation) for introducing me to the concept of the Unique Brilliance Zone (UBZ). You use these tools to help summarise what you are really good at in a short paragraph. After two days working in a group and a day's solitary contemplation (in a remote Tuscan villa in September 2010) I worked out my UBZ:

*'To collect and absorb information, connect with people and share and use ideas as a catalyst to bring about change in people and organisations'*

For me this was a revelation because I was not really working to my greatest strength. Since then, I have begun to move closer to my UBZ, hence this book.

## STEP BY STEP TO CLEAR WATER

**Strengths**: Invest a little money in some self-assessment and develop your own Unique Brilliance Zone.

"I'm developing my unique brilliance zone!"

Let's look briefly at the opportunities and threats. This is less about you, more about your environment, which I have already described in depth in the second chapter. The subject is really too broad to consider here and will be very dependent on your circumstances, so I don't want to say much more except that you should take time to list both your opportunities and your threats. As a financial planner I consider my job is to minimise risks, rather than maximise returns, and you should probably be thinking, at least when considering your family's safety and security, along the same lines. Take the time, therefore, to think about these threats and opportunities.

## FINANCIAL

Before we go on to look at the all-important subject of your goals, objectives, interests and values you need to carry out a financial inventory. This should focus on two areas. The first is **numbers**, the nuts and bolts of what you own and what you owe, how much you earn and how much you spend. The second focus is on your **personal attitude to money**, the core of the following chapter.

As a business owner you will have a good understanding of the concept of profit and loss, cash flow and balance sheets. If you do, then this part of the process should be fairly easy because you simply echo in your family and personal life what you do in your business.

It is very useful, at this stage, to set an annual plan renewal date, a date that is a placeholder for your financial plans. It is the date on which you value your assets and liabilities, the date that you set to record your expenditures, and the date, each year, when you renew your plans.

Try to find a meaningful date that has some relevance to your life. If you are a significant tax payer, then selecting a date one month before one of the key tax dates (31 January, 6 April, 31 July, 31 October in the UK) might be a good idea because it prompts you to think about returns, whilst giving you time to get returns prepared before the deadline.

Some choose a birthday, although it may not have much relevance to your actual life. Many choose 1 January, along with

New Year's Resolutions, although once again, this does not seem to be the most successful date in the calendar for reviewing your financial plans. A personal financial review date close to your business year-end date is often a good idea. As the business owner manager, this provides you with the opportunity to review your life, business and personal finances all at the same time.

My business is very steady; the 31 Dec year-end passes by with only a bit of additional administration, so my own family renewal date is 1 September to coincide with the start of the academic year. In September, normality returns after the long summer holiday, where spending goes ex-routine as we head off on holidays, and make one-off purchases for the new school year.

## STEP BY STEP TO CLEAR WATER

**Renewal date:** look at your annual cycle and select an appropriate annual plan renewal date.

### Inventory

Having set a date, start to build your inventory. Your objective is to come up with a set of financial statements as at your renewal date. These statements should consist firstly of a schedule of assets and liabilities, both financial and non-financial, and with a value placed on everything.

Producing financial statements is an important part of financial planning, although for many starting to prepare them is the hardest parts. Templates spreadsheets can be downloaded from the *Living Money* website to help you get started, or use the app to produce your own personal statements and analysis.

You will find you have three types of assets: used assets, free assets and restricted assets.

> **Used assets** are assets such as your house and car. They are non-financial (although they often have significant financial ramifications). Often they will be depreciating assets, such as your car.
> **Free assets** are financial assets unencumbered by tax or other regulations, which can usually be liquidated at very short notice, turned into cash and used for whatever you need.
> **Restricted assets** are, as the name implies, not usually readily-accessible. The most common example of a restricted asset is a pension. Pensions are usually held in some form of trust arrangement and may not even be a part of your estate. Generally, they cannot be easily liquidated and very rarely can they be handed over as a tax-free lump sum, although benefits can be taken from them in various forms.

Your business is a restricted asset. It supplies you with income, is often not easy to sell and is usually not taken into account when assessing your wealth for estate taxes, so worth hanging on to. Generally, you don't want to, and are probably unable, to sell it at the drop of a hat.

Much of the information you require you can, of course, get from bank statements, mortgage statements, your investment manager or custodian, and other easily-accessible sources of information about easily-valued assets. Some assets, however, you need to take a guess at. Your home is the obvious one. Try and be as accurate as possible, though. Look at papers for asking prices of similar properties, or search the web for the actual sale price of similar properties in the neighbourhood that have recently changed hands.

Make suitable adjustments to your estimate of your own home to reflect differences in comparable properties.

To be fair, most hard-to-value assets are probably your used assets, such as your home. In day-to-day financial planning terms the value of your home is of little consequence unless moving is on the cards. However, there is one area in which it helps to be accurate about this, and that is estate planning and inheritance tax, where a way-out valuation could have a significant impact on your estate and inheritance tax mitigation plans.

## STEP BY STEP TO CLEAR WATER

**Net worth:** List your assets and liabilities; subtract liabilities from assets to obtain your net worth.

Build up a schedule of your pension assets (including State pensions). This you may find a little bit more difficult, especially with frozen final salary schemes you may have belonged to in days gone by. Although it is useful to have an idea of the value (easy for a money purchase scheme, not so easy for a final salary scheme) at your review date, a more important piece of data is the potential income (and cash sum) you might get from the pension, when it might be payable and whether it escalates or not. Even this is less clear these days, as you now have the option of retaining the pension fund beyond 75 without having to draw on it.

In practice, though, what you are really trying to ascertain is your income from pensions at a given age in the future. A quick bit of work on a spreadsheet, taking into account contribution levels, investment returns, annuity rates, inflation etc should give you an idea of what you might get as an income in real terms at a chosen point in the future. When making assumptions about growth rates, remember that you will need to de-risk the portfolio as you get nearer the date you take benefits to avoid a fall in value due to stock market volatility, and this will reduce your overall growth rate.

Next, look at your insurance policies.

## STEP BY STEP TO CLEAR WATER

**Insurance:** create a schedule of insurance policies, listing the premiums, the benefits and payment triggers.

Provide an answer to these questions:

> If I died tomorrow, how much money would my surviving spouse / children receive, and how long would it last them?
> If my spouse or partner died tomorrow, what would I get, and would it be sufficient for my needs and those of my children?

Then ask the same questions about what would happen in the event that you become seriously injured?

**Cash flow**

Next, create a schedule of income and expenditure. This can be a bit more complicated than your assets and liabilities. Remember that you are creating a snapshot of your income and expenditure for the year commencing on the day you have chosen for your planning date. For both, therefore, you are going to have to make some assumptions and projections.

For the moment we are going to concentrate on your current cash flow. However, once you have developed clear goals for your life and costed them out we are going to develop this concept into a lifetime cash flow.

Your income is the area in which you have a close interaction with your business. You will have a number of tax efficient strategies for withdrawing money from your business, including salary, dividends, pension contribution and the repayment of director's loans. If your business is well-developed, and you have planned well, you may already have a clear idea of how much you will pay yourself over the next 12 months, and in what form. If your business is more volatile or you have serious development plans it may be more difficult to predict your income.

Try also to look at this from another viewpoint. Ask yourself 'What must my business pay me in order to live the lifestyle I want?' Take note again of Michael Gerber's principle that your primary role as a business owner is to create more life for yourself, and this should be factored into your business planning.

Record gross incomes and linked expenditures. For instance, when recording income from residential property investments set down the gross income, and list related costs such as letting fees, management and other charges under expenditure. This will ensure you have a clear idea of the profit or loss on your investment property, and are able to subject individual charges to scrutiny.

## STEP BY STEP TO CLEAR WATER

**Income**: set down all your gross annual income and calculate the total.

It is rare that families are able to draw up an accurate and complete list of their personal and family expenditure. Expenditure really gets to people. Often they simply freak on being requested to produce an expenditure statement. Quite often their response will be to say it equates to their income. I always encourage them to dig a bit deeper, partly because it is important to understand where your hard-earned money is going, especially if it is going on purchases that have no relevance to your life goals. Also, it is important that you switch your mind set from *budgets* to *spending plans*. The former implies you are flying by the seat of your pants; the latter implies you have goals and objectives, you know how much you are going to spend and on what. In other words, you are in control.

People have difficulties with spending for practical and emotional reasons. For many, monitoring and managing spending is a chore too far. With everything else going on in their world collecting and recording till receipts, analysing credit card bills, reconciling and checking bank and card statements is just not on the radar, which is a pity because it is profoundly liberating, as Lianne discovered.

However, the Herculean obstacle for many people is the emotion around expenditure. When you start to monitor your spending you hold up a mirror to your life. You see where the money is going – and more importantly, where it is not. This can precipitate real emotional pain if much of your hard earned income is simply going on existing, paying the fuel bills, food bills, the mortgage plus a few impulse buys and some comfort spending that is of no real help in achieving your goals.

Even if you don't know what the figures actually are, you may well already have an intuitive sense of what's going on here. You may experience a nagging feeling that things are not quite right.

For some, ignorance remains bliss and they take no further action, trapped by their fear. Others make a conscious decision to get to grips with their expenditure. They bite the bullet, swallow the frog, travel through the dark wood, however they want to express their journey. They get to grips with their expenditure and start to sleep at night.

## STEP BY STEP TO CLEAR WATER

**Expenditure**: Assess your attitude to expenditure. Are you in control or out of control? If you feel strong emotions of guilt or anxiety don't beat yourself up. Don't judge yourself. Gently and with compassion, decide to take action to gain control of your spending.

71

I devote a whole chapter later to developing plans for spending your time and money, and for ensuring that you stick to those plans. Indeed, this is at the heart of financial life planning and there are many tools and techniques for helping you with this.

**Key personal financial ratios**

So now you have in front of you an entire set of financial statements setting out your current financial situation. Is it good, bad or are you not sure? One way to find out is to calculate some key personal financial ratios[10], much as you would do in your business. Here are a few:

> **Liquidity**: do you have a security or emergency fund? How many months expenditure will it cover? Is this sufficient in the context of the security of your income and insurance arrangements?

> **Savings ratio**: how much of your household income is saved each month?

> **Savings to income**: what is the size of your savings relative to your income? The figure should grow throughout your working life.

> **Debt to income**: what is the size of your debt relative to your income? The figure should fall throughout your working life.

> **Debt to assets**: what are your liabilities relative to your total assets and liquid assets?

> **Debt servicing costs**: what are your debt serving costs relative to your net income?

---

[10] I am grateful to Charles Farrell for introducing me to this concept through his article *Personal Financial Ratios: An Elegant Roadmap to Financial Health and Retirement* published in the Journal of Financial Planning, January 2006.

> **Debt servicing reserve**: how many months' debt-servicing costs are covered by liquid assets?

Once you have spent an hour or so calculating these ratios decide how you feel about them. Consider what they tell you about your ability to achieve your goals and your short and long-term financial security. Give them a red, amber or green flag. The resulting picture will give you a good idea of the health of your finances. Whether that picture is good or bad, one effect of this exercise should be to give you a sense of relief at knowing where you stand. If it is good, you can build on it quickly and start to expand your boundaries. If it is bad, then at least you now know this and can start to take remedial action, which might involve contracting your boundaries in the short term.

This voyage of financial discovery entails a lot of hard work and probably not a little pain and anxiety. However, it is a necessary step on the road to an efficient financial plan, and is part of the planning journey, an exercise that starts to bring about your transformation and a sense of freedom before you have even begun to plan. Remember, it is as much about the process as the plan itself.

## CONVERSATIONS CHANGE LIVES

Before we move on to your vision of the future I want to mention the greatest tool you have at your disposal to help you discover yourself: conversation. I find in my practice that giving time to clients to sit down in our offices (which are secure, peaceful, a million miles away from the hurly burly of life – which is why we make our clients come to us) and talk about all these things is deeply transformative, often in the most remarkable and inspiring way. Whilst exercises and tools are all very well, and in fact give a good grounding to get things going, the real voyage of self-discovery comes in conversation with another. It is this opportunity to express your thoughts to someone else, to have your ideas challenged or supported, to have arguments and assumptions verified or dismissed, that really helps you discover who you are.

So to whom do you talk? Well, family, friends, professional connections, your mentor, are all obvious choices. However, enrolling on a retreat or boot camp can be even more valuable. Over the years I have realised the value of getting out of the home and office for a week or more at a time, mixing with like-minded people whom I have often never met before, to spend time exploring myself and my life, with the help of others (whom, hopefully, I have also been able to help). This is what I call 'travel with a purpose', or transformative travel, a concept I develop in Chapter 11. These should not be technical or skills courses. They should be more strategic in nature, a business or spiritual retreat where you can examine your business and life in deep detail.

My own experience of this sort of travel has been life-changing. I flew to Boston in 2006 and 2008 to attend a five-day, and then a six-day, programme with George Kinder, author of *The Seven Stages of Money Maturity* and a trainer and mentor to the global life planning community. The first involved pairing with Phil Dyer, an US ex-service man turned financial planner whom I had never met before. We life-planned each other and at the same time learnt the EVOKE process. During the five days we delved deeply during structured sessions as well as informal discussions. We talked, we mulled over ideas, set goals and objectives, dealt with obstacles and developed personally in a way that would not have been possible had we stayed at home.

The second retreat was longer, a little larger, more international and once again involved deep personal explorations through conversation. My planner Phil was on the same programme, as was another planner, Lisa Kirshenbauer. After that, Phil and Lisa joined forces and formed a business called Total Business Transformation and I had the honour and privilege of attending their first TBT retreat at the wonderful Torre del Tartufo villa in the remote Tuscan hills. Once again, being away from home and office provided real quality time to think, plan and discuss our lives and businesses with others, to all our benefit.

These retreats, and others, were invariably fun, searching, a little scary at times and a rich source of friendship and support. The point is that conversations are the really important elements of retreats.

## GOALS

Financial planners love to talk about 'goals' because they tend to refer to the achievement of specific events by a specific time, such as stopping work by age 62. It then becomes relatively straightforward to convert these into financial goals and develop sound financial recommendations to achieve them.

However, I believe 'goals' goes much deeper than this. 'Goals' is shorthand for 'goals, values and interests[11]'. And even the word 'goals' in this phrase is not really quite right. It implies something too rigid, too short term and fixed for something so large as, say, bringing up the children.

So I prefer the phrase 'personal projects' popularised, I think, by Professor Brian Little. These could include personal projects such as the children, the home, philanthropy, personal development and education, one's own business, looking after mum and dad in their old age.

---

[11] Lee, Robert and Lawrence, Peter. *Organizational Behaviour – Politics at Work*, Hutchinson, London 1987

Personal projects are different from goals. They are often event driven and they tend not to have a specific target or a specific ending and so, I think, are a better reflection of real life than 'goals'.

Our values will often have an effect on our finances. Most of us don't set down the values we want to live by. We don't have a formal values statement. Instead we live our values instinctively. However, living by values such as integrity, stewardship, hospitality and balance will have a significant impact on our plans.

Finally 'interests' refers to our very deep personal needs and drives, which could include the need for security, love, recognition, status or community and have a significant impact on our finances. There is more about interests in the Postscript to Chapter Ten.

Your goals, values and interests come together in your vision of the future that you will build on the foundations of your life and

money you have just created. What is most profoundly important to you? What values do you want to live your life by, and what impact will those values have on your financial plans? What do you want to achieve? How do you want to change the world? What impact do you want to make on your family, friends, clients? What do you want to have? What must you do? Who do you want to be?

The last question is the most important. I remember in my early days as a peddler of financial products being trained on how to sell an investment plan. The trick was to ask your customer to visualise something they really wanted to have in later life, such as a yacht, a second home or a performance car. Fortunately, we are a little more sophisticated than that now, and we talk to people about goals and objectives. In the main, we are asking our clients about what they want to do with their lives. As the financial life planning movement gathers momentum and wisdom I see the primary question we ask our clients changing to 'who do you want to be?' This goes right to the heart of why we are here on this earth. It meets the growing demand for a more spiritual, compassionate life, a life very different from the materialism of the last few decades. If we can answer this question, and align who we are with whom we really want to be, then we will live lives of deep integrity, at ease with ourselves. And once we have answered this question, the answers to what we want to do and have will follow on naturally.

Demand for this sort of understanding is growing and there are many out there able to provide it, from the monks at Ampleforth Abbey near my home who run regular retreats for non-believers as well as members of the local Catholic community, to the growing cohort of life coaches practising in the country.

If we are going to change the way we are going to live our lives we must address our finances as well as our lives. The other side of the coin is as true, that we cannot really manage our money without having a clear idea of what we want it to do for us. Money is our servant, the fuel we use to drive our lives. As with a car, we don't fill up with fuel because we like petrol. We fill up the tank to get us from A to B. Although the same should apply to money, we have fallen into the habit in recent decades of acquiring money for the sake of it, to boost or massage our egos, to make more money out of money and not simply to fund our lifestyle and meet our true goals.

**Essential personal finance**: an individual who sees money as an end in itself will measure portfolio performance by how much it has beaten a benchmark or an index. The individual who sees money as simply a means to live a fulfilled life will measure portfolio success by the degree to which it helps her to achieve her life goals.

A well-thought-out vision of the future is important for a number of reasons. Most obviously, it provides a destination. If you know where you are going, you can plan a route to get you there, a more direct road to a fulfilled life than the 'if you don't know where you are going any road will take you there' or 'when you get to a fork in the road, take it' approach.

**Essential personal finance**: goals give you energy, vigour and courage to get out of your comfort zone, do things that you wouldn't otherwise do. A clear vision will help you deal with obstacles. The life planning community calls the process of setting goals 'lighting the torch', the result of which is a 'torch statement' that provides light, direction and energy.

At the core of my torch work with clients are three questions that I ask in the Utopia meeting. However, I encourage clients to carry out some deep preparatory work before then, to provide an opportunity for buried memories and desires to rise to the surface and for more detailed, deeper and profound goals and values to emerge. Here are some of the exercises worth doing (some of which you will no doubt have done before).

> **Memories and stories.** Look back on your life (including photos, home movies, diaries), and things you have done, places you have been, people you have been with. When were you really happy? When did you do great things? Would you like to be back there again (or a similar situation)?

> **Landmark events.** Recall a seismic event from your past (either good and bad). Write a letter from that time to yourself today describing the event, how you handled it and how you expect it to change your life. Then write back to yourself in the past describing what has actually happened. Repeat with other events.

> **Role models.** Look at public and private figures you admire and think about why you like them. Describe the values and actions that make them role models.

> **Values.** List the important values you live by, or aspire to live by.

> **Spirit of place.** Think about what you want your ideal home to look like. Where it is, its size, shape, style, layout etc. More importantly, how does your home feel. Who is in it? Is it quiet, peaceful or lively, full of people and children? Having painted a picture of your ideal home (possibly literally) ask yourself whether in fact all you are doing is building a gilded cage. If so, you might want to fast forward to Chapter 9.

> **Your eulogy**. Write about how you want people to talk about you at your funeral.

Now, work through the following three questions[12]:

> The first deals with *getting*. To your surprise, you win the lottery. You now have enough money in the bank to not have to worry about money. How would you spend it? What would you buy? How would you use it?

> The second deals with *doing*. You are talking with a teenager about what to do with a year off between school and university. Suddenly, the teenager turns the conversation and asks you what you would do now if you had a gap year. How do you respond? (Assume all your work responsibilities are taken off your hands, that you have sufficient funds and list what you would begin even if you wouldn't finish.)

> The third deals with *being*. Look forward to the eve of your 100th birthday celebration. You are still sound in mind and body, and the local dignitary, who will be making a speech, calls in to ask you some questions about your self. He asks you to describe yourself. In a few brief phrases, set out how you would like to answer.

---

[12] Followers of George Kinder will note my three questions differ from his. This is not a reflection on Kinder's questions, which are well thought out and, importantly, don't shy from asking us to consider our own mortality. However, I wanted to shift the focus onto 'having, doing and being' and also found, in my frequent use of Kinder's three questions with clients, that the emphasis on our deaths to focus our thoughts on our goals could be a vigour drain at a time when it was important to invigorate and energise.

As you go through the responses start to pick out your really important personal projects. Set these out in your own torch statement, dividing this into short, medium and longer term. You may want to draw up individual and joint statements if you are married or in a long-term relationship. Give consideration to how to support each other in the achievement of your individual goals.

Put some detail into your torch. Paint a picture of your ideal day, week, month, year, whatever time frames most suits you. Write down a detailed description of what your ideal life looks like.

Remember what I said earlier about having conversations. These are more important than ever, now. Jotting down answers to these questions in *My Life Book* is good. The best results will come when you start to have conversations about these questions with your family, friends, business partners, advisors etc.

Now that you have finished these exercises, the outcome may surprise you. You might have thought your goals would centre around the material, the beautiful house, the cars, yachts, second homes etc. My experience, as well as the experience of the growing number of financial life planners around the world is very different. We find that our clients' most common personal projects are:

> *'To have a better, deeper relationship with my spouse or partner'*
> *'To have a better relationship with my children, be able to spend more time with them, support them as they grow up, be there for them'*
> *'To be there for other members of my family, particularly my parents as they grow older'*
> *'To have better personal integrity or spirituality; to find something in myself that is deeper, less superfluous. I want to live a life in which I am true to myself, absolutely whole and*

*not living a divided life where my true self and my everyday self are not fully aligned'*

> *'To be part of a community and help that community to develop and grow.'* This may be a small local community, even just an extended family or group of friends. On the other hand it might be a global community, real or virtual

> *'Personal growth and development is very important to me. I want to travel and grow. I need to get out of my comfort zone, whether it be going down to the local adult education centre to learn a new skill, making a cultural or historical 'pilgrimage' or growing by using my skills and resources for the benefit of those less fortunate than me'*

> *'I want to get creative, write a book, play the sax, paint, sculpt, sing, form a jazz band, etc'*

> *'I want to make the world a better place for those who live here.'* Often this is through building a business based on personal goals and values, the products or services of which have the potential to change the world for the better, as well as make a profit and grow value in the business. It also encompasses the growing agenda of environmental issues.

> *'I would like my ideal home'*

What is interesting about this list is that most do require more time than money, which is why financial life planning is as much about time as money.

If we spend all our time earning, there is not much left over for the real stuff. To this end, your life plan is going to address, in detail, the relationship between your time and your money, and valuing your time is possibly the most important part of this, a figure that can, literally, change your life. I will talk about how you can do this in the next chapter.

I am often asked about couples, and what happens when a conflict over goals and values arises. When you look at the list you will realise that this does not happen that often. Spouse, family, children, community are usually very high up on everyone's agenda. I have occasionally come across mini disputes about the home and what that looks like. These are often worked out through a bit of a compromise or more importantly, the love that a husband and wife have for each other, the understanding that love is a verb and is about giving, so that one spouse will give up something because his or her relationship with their partner is of a far greater importance than the place they live or the look of their home.

Occasionally a conflict can lead to an agreed period of separation, not radical or even legal, simply an agreement to go separate ways for a limited period of time. I have one client, a young and artistic couple, one of whom paints, the other one sings. They both like to develop their skills, so have come to an agreement that during the summer one goes on a painting course whilst the other looks after the children, then they swap and the other goes off to choral boot camp.

On another occasion, the outcome of this detailed exploration of a couple's life goals and values brought about a mutual understanding between them that they were not suited to each other, and had very different outlooks on life. Their decision was to separate, and eventually divorce, enabling them to lead their own lives, fulfil their own dreams, live lives of integrity that they were not able to do together.

A couple of other stories will serve to illustrate the power of this exploration. I took one couple through the process recently. They were in their mid-40s with two teenage children. As the conversation deepened she looked up and said *'I wish I were a better mother, wife and daughter'*. Later, in putting together a plan, we were able to schedule more time for her for her roles as mother, wife and daughter.

The final story concerns an American couple, clients of a US life planner. They requested an initial meeting with the planner, who at the start of the meeting asked them, very simply, why they were here. Their reply was 'Well, we are in our mid-50s and all we have to show for it is toys and bling.' In other words, a deep lack of personal integrity and spirituality. They wanted to stop leading lives of pure superficiality and find something deeper to live for.

## STEP BY STEP TO CLEAR WATER

**Time:** This has been about a deep voyage of self-discovery. If you have had a chance to do just some of the work I have suggested you will probably have felt things start to change. So just for your own interest, go back to the 24-hour clock at the beginning of this chapter and ask yourself again, what time is it now in my life? Is the answer different, and if so, why?

### FEAR BANISHED BY UNDERSTANDING

By putting your heart and soul into this voyage of self-discovery you will come up with a good picture of where you are today. More than that, however, you should see yourself beginning to change and grow already. You may start to see your life in a different light. You may have a greater sense of purpose and direction. You should be starting to lose fears you may have had around money and other elements of your life. Fear is a consequence of the unknown and simply by knowing more about yourself you are able to deal with those fears.

................................................

## POSTSCRIPT

As you start to formulate exciting and life-changing – or even world-changing – goals and ambitions, it's important to remember that you need to be on top form to achieve your goals. Particularly if your goals are centred on other people it is important to look after yourself so that you can achieve what you want. Consider putting together your own mini-plan for the care and development of your mind, body and spirit.

Mind, body, spirit is not actually a New Age phenomenon. The concept was devised by St Bernard, the founder of the Cistercian order and Abbot of Clairvaux, the first Cistercian monastery in 1115. Bernard saw humans as made up of the mind, the body and the spirit, all of which needed rest, healing and growth. To this end he zoned Clairvaux into three parts. The library was for the mind, the kitchens and the dormitories for the body and the chapel for the spirit.

It's a good example to follow, and worth planning out in some detail. Your mind plan might include a list of books to read and act on, courses and retreats to attend. Your body plan could include a fitness schedule, food and diet, weight loss or gain, annual health check-ups. Your spirit plan could include meditation, retreats to help understand what provides most meaning in your life, providing help and compassion to others. *'To evolve into spiritual maturity you must become conscious and effective about who you are and what you need spiritually as well as physically. You must be able to bring together your self-esteem and your intuition in order to act from your power'* [13]

................................................

[13] Myss, Caroline. *Invisible Acts of Power*, Pocket Books, (2006), page 121.

# Five

# THE WALL

'Obstacles are those frightful things you see when you
take your eyes of your goal'

HENRY FORD

So, here you are at a unique point in your unique life. This is the
present, the here and now, carefully documented after all your
hard work of self-discovery, no small achievement that definitely
deserves a pat on the back.

Hopefully, you will also have a clear idea of what your future life
looks like, extracted from your work on your personal projects,
values and interests.

The questions you are probably asking yourself now are these:

> Why am I where I am and not where I want to be?
> How do I get to where I want to be as quickly as possible?
> What's stopping me on my journey? What are the obstacles
  in my way? Am I going to go round these walls, over them,
  under them or straight through them?

Obstacles need to be dealt with or else your aspirations will never
become reality. There is a classic scene in the Bond film *GoldenEye*
in which 007 is confronted by a significant obstacle to the capture
of his adversary in the form of a high wall. He deals with it by
hijacking a Russian tank and demolishing the wall in a spectacular
explosion of stone and bricks. Fun and fantasy it may be; it's a great

scene, however, to recall when we are having difficulty dealing with our own real obstacles.

The first place to start dealing with obstacles is your vision for your life, as Henry Ford realised. With a clear destination and a road map, obstacles fall by the wayside. Goals are more than just a list of aspirations; they give you energy, courage and discipline to deal with obstacles.

## A STRATEGIC AND TACTICAL APPROACH

This is where the plan really starts to take shape. As you identify obstacles you will start to develop both strategies and tactics for dealing with them. As Sun Tzu, a Chinese General and military author is reputed to have said, *'Strategy without tactics is the slowest route to victory; tactics without strategy is the noise before defeat'*.

Strategies tend to be long term, bigger picture. I have a number of set piece strategies that I recommend to my clients. For instance, our Keep Warm strategy deals with the hurdles of achieving a comfortable and secure lifestyle in later life.

The strategy here is to save sufficient in pensions to provide a guaranteed real income to pay only for the non-discretionary, core bills in retirement such as heat, light, food and shelter in later life. Note the key word here is 'only'. In strategic terms, we do not want to over invest in pensions because although they attract tax relief on contributions, restrictions and taxes apply to the benefits. The strategy for funding discretionary spending such as travel and hobbies is to use less tax-privileged savings vehicles. The related tactics concern issues such as where to invest, how an investment policy changes as retirement approaches, how to mix pension savings with other less restricted (and less tax efficient) investment vehicles, and how to take benefits from the fund in later life.

## STEP BY STEP TO CLEAR WATER

**Strategy:** identify existing strategies you use in your life and financial affairs.

### THE PATH TO WISDOM

In confronting obstacles, we grow and develop, especially if we take that inner journey through Dante's dark wood. In the *Divine Comedy* Dante, at a difficult time midway through his life, wakes from sleep and finds himself on the edge of a wood. He sees a place of beauty and peace on a far mountain, starts to journey there, and is immediately turned back by wild beasts representing lust, pride and greed. Advised and encouraged by Virgil, his guide on the first part of his journey, he understands that the only way to get to the mountain, which is Heaven, is to travel through the dark wood (Hell), then through Purgatory and finally to Heaven, the top of the mountain where he meets his beloved Beatrice.

So with us: the obstacles to achieving our goals lie in the mind as well as the money.

**Essential personal finance**: Coming to grips with the emotional issues around money is an important part of financial life planning

Dealing with emotional issues around money is a way of learning about ourselves and achieving personal integrity and wisdom, as well as helping to make more mature and better decisions about money, hence my contention that it is as much about the process as the plan.

I learnt this lesson the hard way many years ago. I had just taken a year out to complete an MBA, racking up significant debts in the process to add to my mortgage, encouraged by the stories of how an MBA would transform my career and earning. Well it did, without doubt. I graduated into the 1981 recession, was unable to find any decent employment apart from some freelance consultancy work, and my earnings dropped to near zero. Still suffering from the illusions of fabulous MBA-generated wealth I ignored my own financial situation until my bank manager got hot under the collar, necessitating a trip to the bank of Mum and Dad, a humiliating and shameful episode that did, however, teach me some extremely useful lessons about myself, money and the benefits of embracing pain, not running or hiding from it.

## PAIN

You will have to confront real emotional pain on your journey through your own dark wood, and you will need to understand that, paradoxically, accepting pain brings relief. You may well have already experienced this when compiling your financial statements, especially if you had never done this work before. You might have felt fear, anxiety, anger, envy, shame, even despair. However, if you persevered you will have come out on the other side with a sense of achievement and excitement. Now you know where you are, you can address the issues that arise and see a path to your goals.

### STEP BY STEP TO CLEAR WATER

**Pain:** identify episodes or situations around your money, past, present or ongoing, which have aroused pain and deep emotions (you may want to fire up your support network before embarking on this exercise).

As you identify obstacles and surmount them practically and emotionally, as you develop strategies and tactics for achieving your goals, as you discover more and more about yourself and gain financial wisdom, you will start to compile an action list. This is your all-important roadmap to your goals. It will set out things to do and when to have them done by. It is your life and financial plan and it emerges, in the main, through identifying and addressing obstacles.

Dealing with obstacles is about meeting reality head on and seeking the truth about yourself, and that often causes pain and discomfort. To create and live the roadmap to your goals and an authentic life requires you to overcome that pain, which in turn requires dedication to your goals and your true self. Often the best way of dealing with painful issues is to do exactly the opposite of what your instincts tell you; when it's cold, dress down, don't wrap up. When you are over-indebted, talk to your lender, don't run away. In fact, initiate the conversation before they come to you. Any discomfort you experience in dealing with obstacles should be welcomed. It may involve a journey through your own dark wood and as Dante and many others have observed, that is often what is required to achieve the goal.

**Essential personal finance**: in dealing with obstacles it is necessary to revisit your goals and your torch statement, relighting your torch time and again.

Of course it is necessary to deal with external obstacles, especially financial obstacles and the implications of our goals for our longer-term financial security. It is also necessary to confront internal obstacles head on, especially dependency, innocent beliefs, blocks and ignorance. You can harness your emotions by turning back to your goals. When you know where you are going, and when the end is something very important to you, you become energised, imaginative, creative, able to overcome practical, financial or emotional obstacles.

---

## STEP BY STEP TO CLEAR WATER

**Goals:** Revisit your goals. Paint a picture (literally if you have that skill) of what your life looks like, and have it always present so you can see it every day. Somehow, somewhere, make sure you connect with your vision of the future every day.

### CHANGING HABITS

This move from where we are now to where we want to be involves change. For many, change is fearful and painful even though, especially in the context of a life and financial plan, it is the dynamic that leads to fulfilment. Embracing and celebrating change needs to be written into your plan.

Life, though, is often a succession of habits, some good and some bad. Moving out of those habits involves moving out of a comfort zone and this is what causes pain. However, good habits lead to improvement, self-development and excellence, something that is common to all plans. We all want to become better at what we do and who we are.

Aristotle understood this over two millennia ago. He wrote that *'excellence is an art won by training and habituation. We do not act rightly because we have virtue or excellence, but we rather have those because we have acted rightly. We are what we repeatedly do. Excellence, then, is not an act but a habit.'*

In her remarkable and iconoclastic book *Quiet*[14], Susan Cain explains the concept of Deliberate Practice, a phrase coined by research psychologist Anders Ericsson and which he sees as the key to exceptional achievement. In effect, this is improving what you do and who you are by habitual repetition.

Much of our life is repetitive, habitual. Change often involves letting go of some habits and taking up others that will lead to a better quality of life.

James Prochaska and his colleagues carried out detailed research into personal change, particularly around quitting bad habits. They concluded that successful personal change is not just about planning and willpower. It is a process, and if change of any form is an important element of your plan then an understanding of that process, set out in their book *Changing for Good*[15], will be of real help. Prochaska identified six stages to making personal change: pre-contemplation, contemplation, preparation, action, maintenance and termination. The insights that he and his team made were to identify the most appropriate tools to use for each stage.

In the next chapter on time and money I recommend habitual practices for recording expenditure of time and money. As habits, these are often resisted for a variety of emotional and practical reasons. However, taking the steps to incorporate these habitual practices in your life leads, ultimately, to improved use of both your time and money – and a more fulfilled life.

## PRACTICAL HURDLES

Practical hurdles to achieving your goals tend to be shaped by your situation and circumstances, and I set down some of these in Chapter 2.

[14] Cain, Susan. *Quiet*, Penguin Books, London, 2012
[15] Prochaska, James et al. *Changing for Good*, Harper Collins, New York, 2006

## STEP BY STEP TO CLEAR WATER

**Practical hurdles:** list out the things that are frustrating you in your search for a fulfilled and happy life. Try to be specific. Instead of simply saying 'I don't have time' say 'I don't have time because…'.

The solutions are often found in improved personal organisation and administration, time management, project management and other transferable business skills.

It is important to put a value on your time. If we cannot put a value on our time, how do we know if we are spending it wisely? Once you know the value of your time you will be able to make informed decisions about what you should be doing, and what tasks should be delegated to others.

As a family entrepreneur, it is important that you spend your time at work and at home in the most efficient way. To do so, your time needs to be given a monetary value and one way of doing this is to calculate a market-based valuation.

This method has its advantages, particularly for anyone in a consultancy or advisory role whose business model is to sell their hours for pounds. It takes as its starting point the comparable earnings for an employed individual in a similar role. The recruitment advertisements should provide a reasonably accurate figure. Then simply multiply this figure by 0.003.

This factor turns an annual salary into an hourly rate for doing the work (x0.001), which is then uplifted once to cover overheads and once again to provide a profit margin (x3). This is a simple, effective way of putting a value on your time and setting a rate at which to charge out your time.

"I'm calculating a market based valuation of the time it'll take to get that lot done!"

"What ARE You doing My dear?"

However, for entrepreneurs intent on using their business to support their own desired lifestyle, this system has a serious flaw, namely, that the market rate bears no relation to their own earnings requirements.

For that, a goals-based method of valuing time is much more relevant and personal and the most common methodology is that pioneered by Dan Kennedy[16] (who provides much good advice on

---

[16] Dan S Kennedy. *No B.S. Time Management for Entrepreneurs*, Second edition, Entrepreneur Press (2013)

time management). If you know that you want to earn £200,000 a year, for example, by doing some simple number work you should be able to see what your time is worth on an hourly basis. And knowing what your time is worth will help you to see when you are wasting it.

Say, for the sake of argument, you feel comfortable working 40 weeks a year, four days a week, five productive hours a day, a total of 800 hours a year.

You have costed out your desired lifestyle, and know that you need to bring home £100,000 per annum. For the sake of argument, double this to £200,000 pa to offset tax, savings, expenses etc (see Chapter Seven below). £200,000 divided by 800 is £250 per hour, the value of your time.

---

**Essential personal finance**: when you know the value of your time you can make informed decisions about what to do.

---

The key here is to know exactly what you are worth, and work at that level. Once you have worked out how to spend your time most productively, this information can be used to put together a time plan to help you deal with practical obstacles (and the emotions surrounding them). More importantly, from a business and personal management point of view it provides the key figure that will clarify what you should be doing and, just as importantly, what you should not be doing.

As a side issue, ask yourself about holidays. If you are employed the maximum amount of holiday available is a key consideration. The holiday question is 'How much holiday am I entitled to each year?' As an entrepreneurial family, however, your attitude will be very different. You will be asking yourself 'How much time do I want to spend at work?' – and hence how much time I want to have at leisure.

## STEP BY STEP TO CLEAR WATER

**Time value:** put a monetary value on your time.

### MONEY HURDLES

If you had unlimited cash you could do what you like, you would be extraordinarily happy and would have no worries. Sadly, we know this is not generally true. It is more an illusion and a fantasy to be replaced, when money does eventually arrive, with the fear of losing it. This is the fear and greed that drives stock markets to the detriment of investment performance. However, we do live in an environment of scarce resources. Time and money are in short supply and here is the interesting bit. If you have worked out your personal projects you will probably realise that these involve time and relationships rather than buying and things. You will begin to realise that you don't need massive resources of capital or income to achieve the majority of what you want. In fact, you may well have sufficient capital and income to achieve much already; you just don't know it because you don't see the picture in long-term, strategic terms.

Having said that, your goals may well be much more outward-looking that just your close circle, and may be centred on compassion and humanitarianism. If this is the case you may obviously want and need to build considerable wealth with which to change the world; this will require a different form of plan, although the principles of financial planning still apply.

If resources are limited, they are not non-existent. Buying a house, educating the children and looking after the senior generations are all areas where intergenerational transfers may be appropriate. Of course, everyone gets very concerned about this.

Questions are asked about value, lifetime financial security, fairness, worthiness and every other concern under the sun, and indeed these are legitimate questions. However, I also believe, firmly, that making sound, considered and reliable plans for the family wealth is a strategic duty, one probably to be initiated by you.

I know from experience that this does not happen nearly as much as it should. Tales of families where no estate planning has been done are rife, sadly. I know of families where a lack of understanding and deep emotions around money have led to parents retaining significant wealth, more than enough to have ensured their lifetime financial security, only on death to have left estates that resulted in significant payments to the Exchequer of inheritance tax, money that could have been used for their own benefit, the benefit of their family and of the wider community.

The ultimate source of resources, however, has to be your own passions, skills, insights, intelligence and drive. Your ability to take an idea and turn it into a profitable business even in the most difficult times will be your true source of wealth. It is no coincidence that one of the earliest business books written was entitled *Think and Grow Rich*[17]. It is also the reason why your spending plans should include a substantial sum for personal development. There is no point in re-inventing the wheel. There are many sources of learning to help you turn your idea, your passion, into a profitable business. Put money aside in your spending plans to make use of them.

When it comes to monetary obstacles, beware of the three Bs – beliefs, blogs and banners.

**Beliefs** and values about money get hammered into us, especially in our childhood, by our parents and grandparents, our elders and

---

[17] Hill, Napoleon. *Think and Grow Rich*, Random House, London, 2004

betters. My grandparents would never, ever, borrow money, and they fed this message down to my parents. My parents bought a plot of land in a village in Yorkshire and built a house a few years before retirement. They had enough money saved up, just not quite enough for their dream house. They could have borrowed the last 10% they needed without any problems, and with inflation rampant at the time, the debt would have reduced in real terms to virtually nothing in a very short time. It could have been repaid from my father's pension lump sum or from a later inheritance. As far as

"This house is 10% too small!"

Mum and Dad were concerned though, you didn't borrow money, and that was that. Within a few hours of moving in to their new house, my mother and father became deeply frustrated that the house was 10% to small, and remained frustrated for the remainder of their lives (frustrations that led to an ongoing battle for more room with the constant addition of outhouses, conservatories, green houses and other add-ons that never quite did the trick and made an otherwise fine house look rather ramshackle and ugly).

The story of my parents' house is all about beliefs that are often planted in our psyches in childhood by other people. They may be correct at the time, or they may be a result of their own prejudices and values. The fact is these beliefs may be faulty, possibly even downright dangerous.

## STEP BY STEP TO CLEAR WATER

**Beliefs**: set down some of your beliefs about money. Analyse them objectively and look at the impact they have had on your financial decisions and security.

Often beliefs are there for our personal protection and comfort. They help to protect the ego and so lead to a cycle of suffering comprising innocence and pain, as George Kinder so eloquently describes it:

'*As we grow out of childhood and the original wholeness of Innocence fades, we take up beliefs regarding money as a way of holding onto what we are losing. Beliefs allow us to cling to an idea of the world as it should be. Of course, the world isn't the way we would like it; it sends us continuous, disturbing, even tragic reminders that it is something other than what we imagine or wish. Pain is our Innocence besieged – the disjunction between what we believe out of our desire to cling to childhood and the reality we must confront'.*[18]

An ingrained belief that may have protected you in the past just brings pain as the cycle gets deeper and harder to break. You get your credit card bill, and it's a bit steep, so you decide to indulge in some retail therapy to ease the pain. You head for the shops, although you only buy what is discounted so that you can head home saying you saved so much by sticking to the sales and bargain counters. None the less, you are still spending money and, what is more, putting it on the same credit card because you don't have to pay now. And then, of course, in a month's time you get the next card statement, which shocks you even more, you go out with your friends for a comfort evening, the drinks goes on the card and the cycle starts all over again.

Why are **blogs** such a danger? It goes back to our earlier discussion about communities and trust. You might read a blog or an article, see a YouTube video, or read a book that tells you that this is a good way of managing your money. Especially if the author seems to have some credibility in the market place you believe what you read and follow the advice, which may turn out all right, or may not.

Ask yourself why the author has written those words. What is his or her underlying agenda? Does he or she really know what they are talking about, or are they just trying to get their name up in lights? Do they suffer from the same innocent beliefs as yourself, and are trying to justify their (and your) actions? A blog or article

---

[18] Kinder, George, *The Seven Stages of Money Maturity*, 1999, Dell Publishing, New York, p73

may be deeply seductive if it pushes buttons for you because it justifies your actions, even though you probably know, deep down, that it is wrong. However, you leap on it because it reinforces and justifies your own innocent beliefs as someone addicted to alcohol leaps on a story about medical research that finds some alcohols are good for you. Although you feel your personal integrity come under strain, because a well-known blogger or journalist has built an argument on the back of their own immature, childhood beliefs that seem to justify your actions, you lap it up and run with it.

Indeed, you should be asking yourself about me, the author of this book. What is my authority for writing this book? What are my credentials, what is my agenda? (The answers to all these questions are, I hope, in the introduction).

The Internet gives everyone the opportunity to publish today, and there is no shortage of people willing to express their opinion for one reason or another. Before acting on their opinion, ask yourself some meaningful questions first.

**Banners** refers to advertising. A well-constructed advertisement that hits your sweet spot can destroy a well-constructed financial plan in the blink of an eye. You probably already know this from experience, especially if your house is littered with objects bought as a result of a particularly smart advertising banner, objects that got used once or twice, then gathered dust.

Practical obstacles can usually be dealt with quite easily, with a bit of thought, imagination and energy. Financial obstacles are usually dealt with through good financial planning. However, it is the emotional obstacles that are the most troublesome, the childhood beliefs that seemed so reasonable and correct at the time that are now a complete hindrance, like the bombardment of messages that hit us every minute of the day, trying to blow us off course. So how do we deal with these?

## EMOTIONAL HURDLES

We have already touched on emotions as a significant cause of failure to achieve goals. Remember Lianne's story, the divorced mother wanting to take her children to concerts? Hers was a classic example of how our emotions erect barriers to protect ourselves (for which read our egos) from pain and disappointment. For this mother, her primary emotion was fear, and indeed in our early days of working together she talked extensively about her fear of money and her fear of not being able to make her money work for her. This resulted in a cycle of comfort buying at the expense of her children's happiness.

We carry a range of emotions and three in particular affect our dealings with money. These are the powerful emotions linked to our core instincts: envy (food), fear (flight), anger (fight). Your envy of another person's lifestyle may lead you to make purchases of items you cannot afford to make yourself feel better. If you fear confronting a situation, such as a heavily overdrawn bank account or an excessive balance on a credit card, you may avoid dealing with the situation in a mature way, thus compounding the problem as you reach or exceed limits and interest charges mount. In turn, this may lead to the emotions of shame and guilt. Anger can arise in situations relating to money at work, at death, at divorce or theft, fraud or betrayal.

### STEP BY STEP TO CLEAR WATER

**Money maturity:** assess your money maturity by completing the Money Maturity Questionnaire overleaf.

## MONEY MATURITY QUESTIONNAIRE[19]

In the grid below, score yourself on the truth of each statement. 'Very true': 5; 'Somewhat true': 4; 'Undecided': 3; 'Somewhat false': 2; 'Very false': 1. A higher score indicates greater maturity.

|   | Stage | Description | Score |
|---|-------|-------------|-------|
| 1 | Innocence | I no longer live by childhood beliefs, thoughts, stories etc, recognising that they are invalid and misleading. | |
| 2 | Pain | I don't feel recurrent pain around money, or envy of others with greater wealth than me, or anger at having to work for a living. | |
| 3 | Knowledge | I have identified my financial goals, assessed my financial resources and planned my finances; I review frequently. | |
| 4 | Understanding | I know that issues around money need to be dealt with within me and that successfully understanding myself will lead to a personal transformation. | |
| 5 | Vigour | My life is deeply purposeful and energetic. I have passions and goals in life and the energy to act on them. | |
| 6 | Vision | My life is not centred on myself alone; I have a keen interest in the wider community to which I offer my resources and talents. | |
| 7 | Aloha or grace | I give out of kindness or compassion, not out of self-interest or in the expectation something will be returned to me. | |

---

[19] I developed this questionnaire for my clients from George Kinder's model of the seven stages of money maturity, as set out in his book of the same name: Kinder, George. 1999. *The Seven Stages of Money Maturity*, New York, Dell Publishing.

Emotions are there to protect us. Self-preservation, and the preservation of the species, is a constraint that confines us to our comfort zone. They shut the door on exploration, risk taking and personal development and growth. However, there is a process for dealing with these self-preserving emotions, a process that actually helps you feed off their energy.

The first step is to recognise the emotions, to know which ones are active and what they are doing to you.

## STEP BY STEP TO CLEAR WATER

**Emotional recognition:** think back to an emotional situation and retell the story to yourself. Take note of the sensations in your body, where they are, what they feel like. Fear might produce a hot flush, a knotted stomach and other sensations. Once you are able to recognise the emotions and know they are there, you can deal with them, and their harmful consequences if left unchecked

The next step is to break the bond between the emotional feelings and the situation that is causing them. As George Kinder succinctly puts it *'let the thoughts go, let the feelings be'.*[20] This is often accomplished through meditation, which I cover later when considering time and patience. Taking time out to empty yourself of your thoughts, just to be with your feelings is a profoundly

[20] Kinder, George. 2011. *Transforming Suffering into Wisdom*, Boston, Serenity Point Press

liberating experience. It does not necessarily involve spending four hours a day in the lotus position. I personally like to walk. The Romans had an expression for this, *solvitur ambulando*, which translates as '*it is solved by walking*'. I find it particularly useful when I am (metaphorically) lost in the woods. It is difficult to describe, let alone to explain, what happens when you separate the thoughts and feelings. However, it does work and can bring a real sense of being at ease, even peace, whilst at the same time letting your mind precipitate the solution to the problem. Indeed, some of my best ideas come when I am walking, so I always carry my iPhone to record them (and just in case I do get literally lost).

## FROM THE ART TO THE SCIENCE OF MONEY

When you find yourself saying things like 'If I had more money I would…' you may think you have hit a financial obstacle although in fact it may be as much to do with your relationship to money as the money itself. However, techniques such as developing spending plans, making cash flow projections, saving and good asset allocation are important tools in dealing with financial issues, so it is at this point in the book that we move away from the emotional, right hemisphere of the brain across to the practical, detailed left hemisphere. This may come as a bit of a shock and you may want to prepare yourself. However, even though resources seem scarce your left hemisphere will surely find what you need if you are sufficiently motivated by your goals, values and objectives.

## POSTSCRIPT

You are now roughly halfway through this book, so it is probably a good time to pause, reflect – and to start taking action. Action comes in the form of a plan – write it, then live it.

You have now done a considerable amount of work in developing a life and financial plan, so start to formalise it by writing it down. Don't jot it down on the back of an envelope. This is one of the most important documents you will write, so give it the respect and gravitas it deserves.

Start by setting out your current circumstances, including financial statements.

Next, set out your **goals**, dividing them up into short, medium and longer-term goals. Set out life goals first, then use them to set financial goals.

Now set out the **obstacles** you have identified, and those **steps** you have decided at this stage need to be taken to deal with them. These steps form the basis of your action plan.

You may be able to start costing these steps out, although you might need more work here. And remember, one of your action points will revolve around day-to-day living, leading the life you want and this will involve plans for regular spending based on the cost analysis you carried out earlier.

There is much more work to do; however, the second action step is to start living your plan, albeit in draft at this stage. This means managing your time and money, the subject of the following chapters.

# Six

## TIME AND MONEY

> 'Time is money, says the proverb, but turn
> it around and you get a precious truth.
> Money is time.'
>
> GEORGE GISSING

Time and money go together like a hand in a glove. They are inseparable, interdependent and intertwined, though the balance changes over time. When we were born we had a whole lifetime in front of us. In our childhood it seemed as though we had all the time in the world, though no money. Minutes, hours, days had no value because there was, to our young mind's eye, an inexhaustible supply of them. However, money seemed so precious because there were all these things we wanted and we either had to save up our pocket money to get them (which required patience, another life commodity in very short supply) or go begging to our parents, a tactic with no guarantee of success.

However, as we get older the values we put on time and money flip. With our life's end rising over the horizon, with things to do, places to go to, people to meet, the value of our time rises almost exponentially. Money, on the other hand, has less and less of an impact and, in the moments before our death, has no value for us whatsoever. Ironically, the fear that we will run out of money before we run out of life motivates many to hoard more and more and spend less and less so that at life's end we still retain substantial assets which might have been better off being recycled and put to better use many years before.

> **Essential personal finance**: financial planning will help you to achieve a balance between your time and your money.

The word 'wealth' can be viewed as a contraction of the words 'well health'. Money is not everything. Having sufficient time *and* money to carry out your goals is important, as is having the physical, emotional and spiritual health to do so at the same time.

Time *and* money are our wealth. They are important and they need managing. Many people attempt to manage their money; very few attempt to manage the way they use their time because this is rarely seen as a commodity to be managed. Indeed, arguably you cannot actually manage time. It flows continually in one direction and at exactly the same rate, and short of applying some Einsteinian relativity you can do nothing about it. However, you can manage the way you spend your time.

I can already hear you, especially if you are a creative free spirit, asking why you want you to manage your time and money. Well, the answer is quite straightforward.

> **Essential personal finance**: taking control of your time and money is the route to personal freedom and happiness. Managing your time and money is all about setting boundaries, which might well involve painful emotions, and when those boundaries are set you are free to do what you will within those boundaries.

Developing goals and creating a plan to achieve those goals is all about setting your boundaries. Renewing your plan is about expanding those boundaries, and as a consequence it is substantially about personal and financial growth.

*" This is my self imposed boundary!"*

Setting and sticking to your boundaries deals with the painful emotions around time and money. Deal with these and freedom follows naturally. Peace of mind becomes the norm. You are able to live in the moment free of fear that you money will run out, free of shame that you cannot do what your richer friends are doing, free of envy and an uncontrollable urge to spend money on things you don't really want just to keep up with the neighbours. You will be able to live, rather than exist.

It is the process of planning, rather than the plan itself, which is important. Managing your time and money is precisely this. It is a continuous journey and cycle of measure, analysis, plan, execute, adapt. It is the daily living of your plan and one that achieves your goals and freedom.

## THE VALUE OF YOUR TIME

The real, practical link between time and money comes in putting a value on your time. We looked at how to do that in the previous chapter and you should now be able to say with certainty what each hour and minute of your waking life is worth.

Knowing your hourly worth, especially if you calculated it using the goals-based method, helps you make clear decisions and set priorities. The fact that you have valued your time at, say, £300 an hour does not mean you are engaged in activities that will earn you that much every hour. Sitting in front of a client and physically charging £300 an hour is one occasion where you see a direct and absolute link between time and money. However, heading off for a walk to clear your mind so you can think better might well be worth as much, if not more. Taking an hour out with a blank pad and a pencil to do some strategic thinking is not going to earn you £300 that instant; over the longer term it might have such a significant impact on your business that its growth and your subsequent remuneration works out at much more than £300.

Conversely, entering bills and receipts, reconciling bank statements, even paying bills is definitely not worth £300 an hour, so you should not be doing it. It is a waste of your time; you are not using your time efficiently and even if you think you have insufficient funds to pay a bookkeeper you should still do so because otherwise you are never going to be able to fulfil your dreams.

Outside the work environment your time is still worth £300 an hour. However, you have deliberately limited the number of hours you spend at work in order make time for your life. You can therefore ask yourself the same question at home as you do at work. If my time with my family is worth £300 an hour (which by definition it must be because you derived the figure you need to live your fulfilled life from your goals, including family time) then why are you cutting the grass or hoovering the floor when you could be out with the family doing family things (or whatever is on the agenda for your life)?

## STEP BY STEP TO CLEAR WATER

**Worthless tasks:** list out things you do at home that could be farmed out to give you time for the important and valuable things in life. Who do you know locally who would do these for you (and thus earn a living from them). Be imaginative: cooking and washing up are a distraction (unless cooking is your thing) whilst going out to a restaurant to eat is valuable family and friends time. This list will form part of the action list in your life plan, and the financial implications will become clear in your cash flow plan (see below).

If you subscribe to the premise that managing your time and money is at the core of a fulfilled life then the first thing you need to do is to start measuring your time and money. You cannot manage what you cannot (or do not) measure and in the rest of this chapter I will talk about practical techniques for handling both your time and

"I'm not hoovering this floor – my time is worth £300 per hour!"

money. The process is very straightforward. First, you measure how you are spending your time and money. Next, you plan how you are going to spend your time and money, based on past experience and future goals. Then you monitor your time and money spending plans before finally adapting them (and hopefully expanding them) in the next cycle.

There is one difference, though, between time and money. Time will run out; money may run out. Time is limited. However you play it, there are only 24 hours or 1,440 minutes in a day (and hence a finite if unknown amount of time left in the rest of your life). All things being equal, the pound or dollar you have today will still be there tomorrow if you don't spend it. This distinction is important and has implications for the way we deal with time and money.

However, whether dealing with time or money, bringing control to them is a three-stage process of measure, plan and monitor.

## TRACKING YOUR TIME

Measuring how you use your time is a challenge! Unlike measuring how you spend money, which can always be done at any time using invoices and bank or card statements, tracking time needs to be done at the time. Making a guesstimate after the fact reduces accuracy. However, it is important, as most of us fail to accurately assess how we spend our time.

You need a tool, one that is simple to set up and use, and that can be synched across multiple measuring devices. You may already use one in your business, such as Harvest. Harvest is project driven, rather than time driven and I prefer apps such as Toggl, which allows time entry first, then allocation to a project or category afterwards.

## STEP BY STEP TO CLEAR WATER

**Time tracking:** review the various time tracking methods and pick one that suits you. Start to record how you track your time over the following days and months

" I haven't time for this time tracking tasklet!"

It is worth being disciplined about this, although I do admit it can be a bit of a millstone, especially when you move into tracking personal time, rather than work time. However, keeping it up for just a month or a quarter can be intensely revealing about the way you lead your life. You will build up a picture of how much time you spend at home, at work (and in between), and within each, how much you spend in various activities. What activities you use will depend on your goals for your life. Categories don't have to be complicated, or that extensive. At work, I record hours based on the (revised) E-myth Seven Centres of Management Attention (strategy, branding, finance, management, delivery, sales and marketing). At home, I record time spent in daily living (or household), family, friends, holidays and leisure. I also record time spent on professional development, personal development (or mind, body and spirit which includes time for things such as meditation and fitness training), and travel. Try to align your home time categories with your home spending categories, and your business time categories with your business spending plans. This helps to bring about a more cohesive picture of your life and business.

Regularly run off summary reports, by the day, week, month and year. Since time is a closed system with a fixed number of hours in the year, it makes more sense to report to yourself in percentage terms to tell you what percentage of the day you spent at work, at home, and on various activities. It is quite probable, the first time you do this, that you will be shocked by the amount of time you spend on things that are nowhere near the top of your priority list, although you may have instinctively felt this and been worried by it, in which case your data will simply confirm what you thought you knew. Either way, it should be a relief to know exactly where you stand, not just where you thought you stood. And with this foundation under your belt you can move on to the next stage of planning your time expenditure.

## TRACKING YOUR MONEY

Now start the same exercise for your expenditure. Apps and gadgets for this are more plentiful than for time tracking. I use MoneyWiz, with a linked app on my iPhone and this allows me to record every item of expenditure, whether cash, credit card, standing order or direct debit. We take all the household receipts and log them into our account and so are able to see, using MoneyWiz's reporting system, how much we are spending over any period of a week or more. Other solutions such as iBank and MoneyDance are also available. Choose one that is secure, robust, well backed up, can be synchronised with your phone or tablet, has an easy interface and easy reporting. MoneyWiz is simple and has a very user-friendly data entry interface. It meets the core financial planning requirement of setting and monitoring your spending plans. MoneyDance and iBank have much more functionality should you require it.

It is worth hunting around the various alternatives to find one that suits you. Some are basic, some have all the bells and whistles including asset and portfolio tracking, balance sheet reporting, debt management etc. Most offer a free trial period or a free number of entries before purchase, so you can test the systems. Generally they are not expensive and you usually reap the cost back in terms of value provided in a short time.

Use the help desks and user manuals to become familiar with your chosen system. However, there are two important things to bear in mind. First (assuming you use an electronic system), it's better to record individual receipts on an item by item basis than to upload transactions from your bank account. This is because you can record more detail, and get a more accurate picture of where your money is going. Whatever you do, don't mix the methods. It will take ages to sort out each month when you try to reconcile.

Second, my clients often ask me how much detail they should go into when recording their expenditure. In an earlier chapter I told of my friendly architect and his comment that 'the detail is the building'; that advice certainly holds good here. A more quantitative reason for maxing the detail is this. If you look at your spending and transactions, you will probably find that around 80% of your spending goes through just 20% of your transactions. That being the case the converse is also true: 20% of your spending will be in the remaining 80% of your transactions. The temptation may be to not bother recording the tail. If you leave those out and you could be 20% out on your expenditure and that is a lot of error when you are trying to build a financial plan (of which expenditure is a key element).

## STEP BY STEP TO CLEAR WATER

**Money management:** review the various cash measurement methods and pick one that suits you. Start to record your income and expenditure over the following days and months.

A useful cross check to assess the accuracy of your expenditure records is to look at your assets over the same period. If the value of your assets has fallen and you are recording expenditure less than income then something is wrong. In general terms (ignoring investment growth or loss) if your expenditure exceeds your income your net assets (ie assets less liabilities) will decrease and if your income exceeds your expenditure your net assets will increase.

## TIME AND MONEY SPENDING PLANS

Now you need to return to your goals and use them to develop spending plans for your time and money. However, you need to do this in relation to what you have spent so far. When it comes to the money some items are not, at first sight, changeable. These tend to be the basics relating to your house, keeping secure, warm and fed and watered. However, on the micro level, you can take the opportunity to review and see if you can get better deals on things like gas, electricity and communications.

At a more strategic level, you might want to look at your house, especially as your children start to move away, and decide if the money you spend on your house could be used more effectively elsewhere to provide additional cash to further your goals (which are probably now more in the realm of doing and being rather than having). If that is the case you may want to take a strategic decision to downsize your house.

Planning your time may be a bit more difficult, although the concept of blocking out your time, one you already use probably, is very helpful. However, as a business owner, you will be interacting with other people and may not have full control over your calendar. Even so, you should return to your time valuation exercise and note the number of hours you planned to work in each day, week, and year. If you have planned to work for, say, 40 out of 52 weeks in the year, then at your annual renewal block out those 40 weeks as work weeks. Get them into the calendar and then the remaining 12 weeks are there for you for your personal goals. You can paste in family holidays, or breaks for you and your partner when the children are at school.

## STEP BY STEP TO CLEAR WATER

**Time planning**: buy a large year planner; put it in a prominent position in your house, block out time at work and fill in the remaining spaces with personal activities. Plan and book holidays and travel at the start of the year. If you need to go into more detail on a daily or weekly basis use a spreadsheet or calendar application to allocate tasks to time.

Task management systems such as Remember the Milk are also of great value here. Alternatively, apps like Toggl are very helpful, enabling you to put in an estimated time for a particular project (for which read your core life activity), and a bar chart shows you the amount used as you progress through your year.

"I'm Managing My Time!"

Whilst you are doing this, of course, you will also be costing out your personal activities and putting these into your spending plans.

Whatever system you use should enable you to set up spending plans (or budgets as they are usually called, which I always think that sound very negative), so make use of this and your calendar to set out plans for spending your money and time for the next 12 months – and beyond.

### LIFETIME CASH FLOW

The lifetime cash flow (LTCF) is at the heart of your financial plan. It is where the rubber actually hits the road, so to speak, where your plans over time meet the money that is going to fund them. The LTCF is where your time and money plans merge into a single picture of what your life and finances will look like over your lifetimes.

> **Essential personal finance**: your lifetime cash flow is an invaluable tool in your planning, allowing you to create what-if scenarios to see the impact of how you spend your time and your money, and thus helping you to make informed decisions about your time and money. Most importantly, it balances the achievement of important goals in the short term with lifetime financial security.

Sadly, the concept of the lifetime cash flow, and the tools that help you construct one, are mainly the preserve of financial planners at the moment. However, you can easily construct your own on Numbers or Excel.

So what is a lifetime cash flow? In short it is a model of your money over time. It is constructed by recording details of your current assets, liabilities, income and expenditure and also future events such as retirement, house sales, pension benefits, investment growth, mortgage repayments etc. Once this has been completed, you can see a picture of two important elements of your finances –

the difference between your income and expenditure over your expected lifetime, and the projected value of your liquid assets over your lifetime. The former enables you to see when expenditure exceeds income, and hence when you will need to call on your cash reserves or the bank to fund excess expenditure. The latter will tell you if you are going to run out of money during your lifetime.

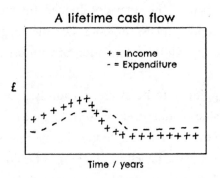

A lifetime cash flow

The lifetime cash flow chart shown here is a classic example of surplus income during working life. This income is saved by the family and is reflected in the lifetime liquid assets chart, which shows a rising value of liquid assets during this phase of life.

With a lower income in later years, expenditure exceeds income and the difference is made up of drawings from liquid assets, which then start to decline.

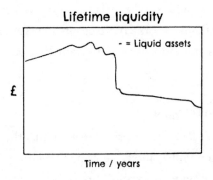

Lifetime liquidity

The liquid assets chart provides the answer to that all-important question about longer-term financial security: *will my money run out before I do?*

It is worth making a few provisos and comments here. The first is that this is only a model, not the actual thing, and the assumptions you make, which determine the shape of the charts, may actually happen, or they may not. Indeed, the model is only as good as your inputs and assumptions. Garbage in, garbage out, so accuracy and thoughtful formulation of your assumptions is important.

The second point is to be aware, obviously, that accurately projecting the value of your assets in 50 years' time is not realistic. So, why go to all this effort? Well, first, remember my story about learning to drive, and the benefits of looking as far down the road as possible? Well this is exactly the same principle. Second, we know one of the main reasons why we plan is to balance immediate achievement of important goals with long-term financial security, and the lifetime cash flow does exactly this. If the model shows you running out of money in the future, you can take steps now to deal with the situation. Conversely, if it shows an excess of capital in later life that may be an excellent reason to widen your horizons, extend you boundaries today.

Plans, like planes and Apollo rockets, get blown off course and need constant in-flight adjustments to ensure they get to the desired destination. It is therefore very important that you update the model regularly.

## MONITOR AND REVIEW SPENDING
Business owners will not be surprised to learn that the final step of this exercise is to monitor and review your spending. That means continually recording your expenditure of your time and money,

as you have been doing already, and monitoring your expenditure against your spending plans.

Your cash planning app should allow you, at a glance, to see diagrammatically your actual expenditure in relation to your planned expenditure over any time period. It will probably use some sort of red, amber, green colour coding so you can see at a glance if you are within your plans, close to the edge or over-extended.

As you get more proficient you will be able to adapt both your processes and your plans, leading to a shift in the way you spend your time and money away from things that don't further your life goals to expenditures that do.

We always think of controlling our expenditure as about not spending. However, the opposite is equally true. If you have planned to spend a certain amount on something that is to do with your goals and you see you haven't spent it, then make sure you do. The system is, in effect, giving you permission to spend time and money on that item or activity. You can do it without guilt that you are overspending or worry that you will run out of money, because it is all planned.

## THE FREEDOM OF BOUNDARIES

This chapter has been all about boundaries. As such, you might now be rebelling, telling yourself that you don't want to be confined and restricted in such a way. After all, you are a free spirited, adventurous, freeformer. Why should you restrict the way you spend your time and money in this way? Boundaries are actually the route to freedom. Boundaries are often imposed on us by society. We are bound, in the UK, to drive on the left hand side of the road. We cannot just cross the boundary into the right hand side. If we did, none of us would get anywhere, except possibly the nearest hospital.

These exercises in planning your time and money are just an extension of this principle, self-imposed boundaries which provide you with a route to freedom. As time goes on, as your business and family grow, as your goals develop, you can narrow some boundaries and expand others. It shouldn't take me to tell you which to shrink and which to grow. What is happening here is that you are beginning to plan how to achieve your most important life goals in the quickest and most efficient way, and that should be a real joy.

## POSTSCRIPT

Although I have emphasised that setting boundaries is the route to freedom, the concept can still seem negative and restrictive, rather like a professional batsman on an undersized country cricket green constantly hitting sixes and wanting to extend the boundaries.

When you renew your plan each year you can take the opportunity to expand your boundaries with more cash to spend, or lower expenses or tasks delegated to create more time. To keep positive about this exercise, think about how you might extend your boundaries. Look five years down the line and consider what a life of freedom might look like then.

## Seven

# THREE FINANCIAL DRIVERS TO FREEDOM

The last four chapters have been about the achievement of your deepest and most profound goals in the shortest possible time. However, this must be done in a way that recognises your longer-term responsibilities. The key objective of financial life planning is meeting your profound goals in the quickest and most efficient way, whilst being responsible for your longer-term welfare and security.

This chapter looks at the three drivers of a financial freedom: saving, compound returns and asset allocation. Out of this will emerge a technique for arranging your finances in an efficient and structured way that will ensure you meet your short-term goals as well as your longer-term security.

### SAVING

> 'A part of all you earn is yours to keep.'
>
> GEORGE S CLASON

We start with saving. Saving it is the route to longer-term security and provides the funds to live a fulfilled life even after you have hung up your working clothes. In conjunction with compounding and asset allocation, saving into real assets such as equities and property neutralises the effects of inflation over the longer term.

However we may also need cash for the short-term. We don't know what will happen tomorrow, even in the next hour. We could be the victim of an accident, a freak weather event, lost luggage, something that needs cash here and now, even if it comes back to you from an insurance company later on. We will occasionally have large expenses, such as paying for a holiday that may be beyond normal monthly cash flow. Tax liabilities also seem to cause trouble and stories of people suddenly realising they have a significant tax bill to pay and no cash to do so are surprisingly common. For these reasons we should also have short-term cash savings, a Security Fund. Sure, it is not going to provide much of a return especially at today's interest rates. It will provide you with a return in the form of peace of mind.

As a business owner, your cash flow may be erratic, to say the least. This is especially the case if you are working on a project basis, a way of working that is becoming more common these days. Probably that is a lifestyle choice, one that you are happy with, and it implies that your earned income will come to a stop every now and then. That being the case you need to have funds available for these intervals. This means your Security Fund will need to act as a buffer and be somewhat larger than a straightforward emergency fund. It will be reasonably easy to access and possibly invested cautiously so that it is not vulnerable to stock market volatility.

However, when we think of saving we normally think of longer term saving. In chapter two I set out some statistics about our longevity – with good reason. We all know we are living longer, so what will be the impact on our lives.

If you are 45 now, do you want to carry on working to 100? Will you be able to at that age? You need to be realistic about the length of time you will be able to work, and the length of time you will want to work. Even if you decide 70 is the cut-off point that could still leave you with further 30 years of life that you will want to live to the full, and that is going to take cash.

Here is a checklist and assessment of possible sources of cash for later life:

> **The State Pension.** How much it will be and when you will receive it is uncertain, and the rules keep changing. With public sector finances under pressure it as likely to go down as up.

> **Insurance policies.** The clue is in the name. They only pay out when things go wrong. As things do go wrong it's important to build in some protection insurance into your plans.

> **Liquidating assets.** Most commonly, downsizing our houses, selling our businesses and selling other properties. These are risky because so much capital is tied up in a single asset. Property does go down in value as well as up and a property may become difficult to sell for some time. I know of one couple who invested heavily in mussel beds in Scotland, only for the beds, and themselves, to be wiped out by lethal algae just before the completion of the sale of a business to an international food conglomerate. However, many do sell businesses and property very successfully.

> **Inheritances.** Don't rely on them. Tax and long-term care costs can seriously damage your potential inheritance.

> **Pensions.** Pensions have a bad name for reasons ranging from Maxwell to investment management. However, I have the privilege of looking after a number of elderly clients. There is absolutely no doubt in my mind that those who saved into a pension during their working lives are now reaping the benefits through the receipt of a real, regular monthly guaranteed income for life. Further, recent changes to pension benefit regulations have abolished compulsory annuitisation and added more flexibility.

> **Savings.** Savings are an excellent source of income and capital (generous capital gains tax allowances allow

significant sums to be withdrawn from portfolios each year free of capital gains tax and other tax-privileged vehicles also lighten the tax burden). Mixing and matching pensions and free assets during accrual and decumulation can lead to considerable tax efficiency. Of course an investment portfolio has to come from somewhere and, like pensions, this will normally involve putting money aside out of earned income – saving.

**Essential personal finance**: in a word, saving is probably the most important route to financial freedom, especially when practised in conjunction with compound returns and asset allocation.

This is why I recommended, back in Chapter 5, that you calculate your key personal financial ratios. The goal-oriented ratios, those which measure your liquid assets, debt levels and your savings rate as the years go by, give a good indication of the success of your savings strategy. The security key ratios are just as important, with the liquid asset ratios and debt repayment ratios dependent on your savings and investments.

## STEP BY STEP TO CLEAR WATER

**Savings:** look at your own financial situation and identify sources of income for later life, assessing the risks to those sources and the potential returns.

So how do you save, and how much should you save? To answer, you need to return to your income and expenditure statements. You need to make some decisions about both in order to get some clear water between your income and expenditure, the difference being money that goes into your savings.

It is useful to think of saving as the purchase of units of investments, to be included in your spending plans in much the same way as you might include the purchase of food or utilities. In our financial statement templates we put this as the number one item.

You also need to look at your lifetime cash flow, and in particular start some scenario planning. If you see that you are already running out of capital by the time you get to 70, say, then start to work up some scenarios that will close the gap. These could be based on the above ideas, and the most fundamental one is to look at your expenditure relative to your income, and whittle back unnecessary spending to create surplus income for saving. If you have done some good work on your vision and goals, then these will be able to tell you whether an expenditure item is a help or a hindrance.

---

**Essential personal finance**: when you make decisions about spending money and creating spending plans ask yourself *'Does spending this money help me to achieve my goals?'*

---

You may, however, like a bit more guidance on the matter of how much to save. A good rule of thumb is to save 10-15% of everything you earn – from day one. Given that you are probably well beyond your first day at work and have not been overly conscientious about adhering to this particular rule, its more than probable that you have not got quite the savings you should have by this stage. In fact, the 10-15% rule is probably more appropriate for your children than you.

Remember that debt repayment counts as savings (whether you reduce debt or increase savings and investments the net result on your balance sheet is the same). Well-managed, long-term debt to purchase a house is perfectly acceptable. It is long-term and there is no requirement, either financially or emotionally, to hasten its repayment. Emotionally, you should give yourself permission to live with long-term debt, permission made much easier if you have a defined repayment plan. Out of your surplus income you should allocate sufficient to debt repayment to meet a target debt deletion day, with the remainder going into savings and investments. If you go down the route of maximising your debt repayment (which you may have to in the short term if it is too high) and neglect savings, then you will have a good balance sheet and no liquid assets. You will be asset rich and cash poor, a very common complaint amongst households in the UK these days.

During the post war period, reflecting possibly that core value of duty, the savings ratio in the UK kept on rising. It stopped rising in the early 90s until it reached a low point in 2008 of 2%. In fact, if you include the increases in household debt and the extraction of equity from property the saving ratio was negative. After the 2008 financial crisis, however, households realised they had to address their high debt levels and low savings, and the savings ratio increased to over 6%[21]. Home austerity is in fashion these days and, although it may be painful in the short term, it is worth bearing in mind that if we as a nation can bring household debt down from its current level to the 30% it was in the 1970s, then our personal and national prosperity is increasing.

A treatise on saving would be incomplete without reference to the key lesson spelt out by Arkad, the richest man in Babylon: *'a*

---

[21] 2nd quarter, 2012. Office of National Statistics

*part of all you earn is yours to keep*.[22] Adapting Arkad's lessons to today, here is how every £100 of income might be used:

- > Tax: £15
- > Savings: £10
- > Tithing (philanthropy): £10
- > Debt repayment: £15
- > Living: £50

Now there is a very different model for living to today's norms.

## COMPOUND RETURNS

> 'Compound interest is the most
> powerful force in the universe.'
>
> ALBERT EINSTEIN

Compounding is what happens when interest (or dividends) on the 'part of all you earn that you keep' are retained in the investment so that the interest itself earns interest to give compound returns, rather than simple returns. As a very simple example, take a cash sum of £1,000 and invest it (and the income generated) at a growth rate of 7% per annum for 40 years. At the end of that time you would get back £14,974 (this is just doing the maths at the moment, so ignore issues like tax and whether you could get a 7% return consistently over 40 years – I will address these concerns shortly).

Compare this to where interest is removed from the investment when it is earned (simple interest). In this case the total we get back

---

[22] Clason, GS. *The Richest Man in Babylon* (revised edition). BN Publishing (2006)

at the end is £3,800 (interest at £70 a year for 40 years, plus the original £1,000).

Compound returns are another example of the interrelationship between time and money. The longer you leave money invested, the greater the returns. Compound interest produces an exponential curve that is upward sloping and increases faster as time progresses. The chart shows the value of our £1,000 invested for 40 years at 7% pa compound.

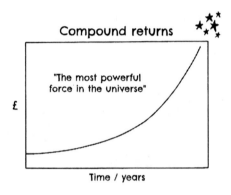

Is this relevant to our day-to-day lives, you might ask. Well, let's say you started work at 25 and, with great foresight, put £1,000 pa in a tax-privileged investment. This could well be left for 40 years until you are aged 65, and 7% per annum is the order of return you might expect from equity investment. So when you looked at your investment on your 65th birthday, it would be worth, in nominal terms, £14,974.

However, let's say you were even more conscientious and, rather than investing one single sum at age 25, you invested £1,000 every year at 7% pa compound, the investment will be worth a few pounds short of £200,000 at age 65.

Of course, it is not quite as simple as this in real life. Things like earnings, taxes, stock market volatility, interest rate fluctuations and shifting attitudes to risk make it highly unlikely that you will get a consistent 7% pa return[23], or be able consistently to save the same amount of money year on year. And we have not mentioned inflation yet. Our examples have all been nominal, not real figures. Inflation compounds in the opposite direction, reducing the real value of your money over time and cutting into the spending power of your capital and income. Indeed, stock market volatility and inflation are the two big risks we have to deal with when we discuss where to invest, as we shall see.

It is more instructive to use a real rate of growth. If we assume inflation at 2.5% pa, then we should reduce our investment return from 7% pa to 4.5% pa. The lost 2.5% simply maintains the real value of the investment over time. The real value of our savings after 40 years is now a more realistic £107,000. In other words, this is the purchasing power of that investment at the end of its life in today's terms

It is a good discipline to think in terms of real money and purchasing power in today's terms. If you do this, long telephone number figures in your calculations will make more sense. Similarly, you can think of investment returns in real and nominal terms. If you think, for instance, that over the longer term you can expect a return of 7% pa from an investment, ask if that is nominal or real. If nominal, convert it into a real return of 4.5% pa (at inflation of 2.5% pa).

---

**Essential personal finance**: in spite of inflation, compound interest is a powerful force. It needs time to work, so the message is *start early*.

---

[23] Indeed, the nearer you get to taking cash, the lower the risk you will need to take, and hence the lower the returns (see the next section on asset allocation).

## ASSET ALLOCATION

'... investment policy dominates ... market timing and security selection, explaining on average 93.6% of the variation in total plan return.'

BRINSON, HOOD AND BEEBOWER[24]

Carl Richards is an American Certified Financial Planner and a cartoonist. Ask him what is the biggest cause of poor investment performance and he will draw this cartoon.

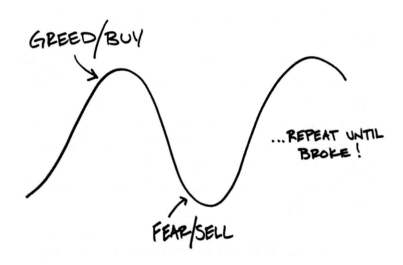

---

[24] From *Determinants of Portfolio Performance*, Financial Analysts Journal, July / August 1986, by Garry P Brinson, L Randolph Hood and Gilbert L Beebower. See below for additional comments on this paper.

His answer to the question is straightforward: more often than not investors themselves have the largest impact on investment performance because the twin emotions of fear and greed lead to investment calls that are almost guaranteed to ensure poor performance.

When making day-to-day purchases, anything from a car to soap, we generally try to find the cheapest price or to negotiate the price down with the vendor. When we sell something, say on eBay, we do what you can to get the best price for it.

With shares, the opposite tends to happen. As the markets and the price per dollar of earnings rise, private investors start to pile into shares, joining everyone else until when the market hits its peak they are running with the crowd, letting their greed have free rein and piling everything into equities or property – at which point they peak. As markets start to fall (as they inevitably do, because they are as cyclical as the seasons), investors start to get worried, even though the investments are probably cheaper relative to their earnings. At the bottom of the market an intolerable fear that everything will be lost takes over and investment portfolios are liquidated at their cheapest.

If am being a little simplistic here there is nevertheless considerable truth in what I say. In 1841 Charles Mackay provided an excellent description of emotion-driven investors during the 1630s Tulip Bubble in his famous book *Extraordinary Popular Delusions and the Madness of Crowds*[25]. History has repeated itself many times since then, right up to the Tech Bubble of 1997 to 2000 in which investors discovered a strong penchant for shares in technology companies, some of which didn't even have revenues.

---

[25] Mackay, Charles, *Extraordinary Popular Delusions and the Madness of Crowds*, Wordsworth Editions, London 1995

**Essential personal finance**: if you don't wish to be your own worst enemy, formulate an investment strategy and stick to it. The most rewarding one will be one based on asset allocation rather than stock selection or market timing. Research shows that, of the three, correct asset allocation far outweighs the others in terms of portfolio performance[26].

Investment strategy is about obtaining the desired result from your portfolio for a given level of risk. Note I say 'result' not 'return', reflecting my view that the objective of your portfolio is to serve you in the achievement of your life goals, not simply to make money.

## STEP BY STEP TO CLEAR WATER

**Portfolio objectives**: consider your own investments and think about what you would like your portfolio to do for you, now and in the future.

---

[26] There is a certain amount of controversy about this research. The original research, carried out by Brinson et al (*Determinants of Portfolio Performance*, Financial Analysts Journal, July / August 1986) showed that for large pension funds investment policy dominates investment strategy (market timing and security selection), explaining on average 93.6% of the variation of the plan return. The authors concluded: 'Although investment strategy can result in significant returns, these are dwarfed by the return contribution from investment policy - the selection of asset classes and their normal weights. Many commentators saw flaws in this research as being too limited and in a subsequent paper (Ibbotsen, Roger and Kaplan, Paul, *Does Asset Allocation Explain 40, 90 or 100% of Performance*, Association for Investment Management and Research, 2000) the authors widened the scope of the question to look at mutual funds. They concluded that '*asset allocation explains about 90% of the variability of a fund's return over time but it explains only about 40% of the variation of returns amongst funds*'.

There are two main risks to your investments: stock market volatility and inflation. **Volatility** is a short-term risk, only if you need money. The risk is, simply, that if you need money from your portfolio and have to sell shares to get that cash when markets have fallen you might end up selling at a loss; at the least, you might have to sell more shares than a month before to raise the same amount of cash.

> - Markets correct frequently, and crash less often, though more spectacularly.
> - The Wall Street Crash of 1929 saw US stocks fall by 38% on 28 October (Black Tuesday) and a further 31% the next day. Between October 1929 and July 1932 the US stock market fell by 89%.
> - During the Crash of 1973 the UK stock market lost nearly 75% of its value as investors ran for cover in the post-Bretton Woods currency crisis and the oil crisis.
> - I recall watching the screens turn red in the City of London on 19 October 1987 (Black Monday) when global stock markets lost a third of their value in a day as confidence disappeared. Coming on top of the previous Friday's hurricane that had hit London and the South East it was a shocking time, though the longer-term chart of the FTSE now shows it to be no more than a short-term correction from an overheated position.
> - During the first two years of the Millennium, markets fell by around 45% as technology stocks crashed and central bank liquidity put in place to minimise Millennium Bug disruption and the introduction of the Euro was withdrawn.
> - The 2007 banking crisis, combined with hugely overvalued shares and excessive debt, led to the most recent crash,

during which global stock markets lost between 45% and 55% of their value.

Markets correct less dramatically and more frequently. Many years will see a brief period during which stocks will fall by up to 10%. Falls of between 10% and 30% occur on average every five years.

On the whole, volatility is a short-term and dramatic phenomenon. In the main it lasts for a year, although on rare occasions volatility lasting seven years has happened. Of course, these figures from the past may not be a reliable indication of the future, and your own attitude to risk may tell you to opt for a more or less conservative approach. However, as a rule of thumb, factoring in volatility periods of between three and seven years during which it might not be prudent to sell equities makes sense.

The central theme of stock market volatility is that asset prices fall and will recover. However, some may not, of course, in which case fall becomes loss, a much more serious situation. This is why, for most people, investing in the stock market through a collective fund where a single stock will usually account for no more than 5% of the total fund makes sense. Collectives provide access to the risk reduction benefits of diversification.

**Inflation** is a long term, serious risk to portfolios and your lifestyle. Over 20 years inflation at 2.5% will wipe 40% of the real purchasing power of your cash. Over 30 years it will more than halve the spending power of your capital and over 40 years it will annihilate two thirds of the purchasing power of your portfolio.

Given current longevity, these timeframes are very real. It is perfectly possible that you will live to 95. If you stop working at 65 your capital and income from other sources will have to last you 30 years and you need to think carefully about how you are going to deal with the impact of inflation on your financial security. Good asset allocation and risk assessment is at the core of the solution to this.

Most people have a single-minded view of risk, namely that in nominal terms their investment will be worth less tomorrow than it is today. However, there are plenty of other risks, such as liquidity risk (or the lack of it), interest rate risk, currency risk, counterparty risk (if you decide to delve into structured products) and gearing risk as well as investment-specific risks such as the quality of a company's management, its capital structure and so on.

Risk and return are inextricably linked, and risk, of course, brings about the possibility of temporary or permanent loss. In financial planning terms, it makes sense to manage risk first, returns second. There are three elements of risk you need to consider: what risk you *want* to take, what risk you *need* to take and what is the *maximum* risk you can take that will ensure you don't suffer losses that will damage your personal financial security (your capacity for loss).

The risk you want and the risk you need are often very different. You may be very risk-averse. If you take this approach with your pension, a very long-term investment, you may never get the returns you need for a secure lifestyle. Your investment horizon could be between 15 and 35 years if you are 40 now. However, seven years is a reasonable length of time for a portfolio to recover in real terms from a severe fall. With a time frame two to five times that recovery period it does not matter if the portfolio falls in the early days. Indeed, if you are investing on a regular basis you simply buy more shares at a cheaper price. However, it is important to de-risk the portfolio as you approach the time at which you take benefits.

Conversely, you might want to take some risk into your portfolio, although your lifetime cash flow shows that this is totally unnecessary as your financial security is strong throughout your life.

So the risk you need and the risk you want are often very different. If the risk you need to take is important, your capacity for loss is even more important. Shortly after one stock market fall I remember a tragic radio interview with a man who had put all his savings into a single precipice bond (equivalent to a bet on a set of indices). He had been attracted by the promise of high returns and been advised that the risk of anything going wrong was very low, which it was. However, the consequence of the risk materialising would be a total loss of the investment. The risk did materialise, the investment failed and he lost everything. To make things worse, his capacity to absorb this loss was very low (these were his life savings and there was nothing else) so the consequences of the loss were devastating.

Arguably, it is your plan that should drive the amount of risk you will take with your portfolio. You should nevertheless have some idea of your own risk return profile (which may be different for different elements of your portfolio).

## STEP BY STEP TO CLEAR WATER

**Risk assessment:** use the following questions to assess your own attitude to risk.

> Do you consider yourself to be financially savvy and experienced?
> In emotional terms, what does *risk* mean to you? Is it something to be embraced because of its potential returns, or to be avoided because of the potential losses? Is greed or fear your dominant emotion? Is your concern more with the losses or the gains?

> Recall some of your past investment decisions. Do you consider yourself to be a low, moderate or high-risk taker? Has this changed over time?

> Do you think of risk in terms of falls or losses? What level of fall or loss in your portfolio would stop you sleeping at night? 10%, 20%, 50%?

> Which do you consider to be the greater risk: short-term stock market falls or long-term loss of purchasing power due to inflation?

> What mix of the main asset classes (cash, fixed interest, equities, property, alternatives) would you be most comfortable with in your portfolio?

> What sort of return would you expect from such a portfolio?

Investment strategies enable you to achieve a desired result from your portfolio for a given level of risk through the process of allocating capital to the main asset classes (cash, fixed interest, equities, property and alternatives) in a way that will ensure you always have the right money in the right place at the right time. The characteristics and the risk return profile of each asset class is therefore important and what follows is a brief and very simplistic description of each (so further exploration through more comprehensive texts is recommended).

**Cash** is reasonably straightforward. It is highly liquid, in the main instantly accessible (unless it is on a fix) and has low returns, especially in the current low interest rate environment. Cash loses its value in real terms over time, especially if interest is withdrawn or is lower than the rate of inflation. Cash is a nominal asset, one with a fixed value that does not change. £100 today was £100 yesterday and will be tomorrow (in nominal, not real, terms). The rate of interest you obtain can depend on the length of time you commit the money, the amount of your investment (larger sums generally attract higher rates) and also the creditworthiness of the institution holding your money.

This later point deserves some attention. As I have already said, return and risk are related. Given that there is no such thing as a high-return, risk-free, tax-efficient investment any unusually high interest rate should act as a warning bell. I will never forget the disappointment of a friend who, back in the 1980s, placed a considerable sum on deposit with the Bank of Credit and Commerce International. When I asked him why (given that the rumours flying around the world were already rampant) he told me it was because they were offering the best interest rates on the market, which they were – and in 1991 the bank was shut down in a global operation by financial regulatory authorities. He received a small pay-out some many years later, and in effect said goodbye to £30,000.

**Essential personal finance**: cash is highly liquid, vulnerable to inflation and generates low returns. Its liquidity is its strength, which is why it is an important component of an investment portfolio.

**Fixed interest investment** is a little more complex. Like cash, it is a nominal asset, though with the potential for better yields and limited capital growth. Fixed interest investments are also known as bonds. Unfortunately, this term applies to a wide range of financial products, including some life insurance policies and even, in some parts of the world, mortgages. There is a reason for this, which is that all these instruments involve some sort of promise or a defined return in return for the payment of a premium of some kind. However, for the sake of brevity I am going to refer to the fixed interest investments under discussion as bonds, on the understanding that my remarks apply only to these types of investment.

Bonds can be issued by governments (known as government bonds, sovereign debt or, in the UK, gilts, because they were printed on gilt-edged paper and regarded as the soundest investment), local or regional authorities and by companies (known as corporate bonds). For all these institutions, issuing a bond is one way of financing their operations. Bond issuance sits between overdrafts and equity funding (for a company). The essence of a bond, in very simple terms, is this: an institution wishes to borrow money so it sells to investors a block of bonds. Each bond has a face value of £100. The deal is that the institution promises to pay, for example, interest of 5% on the face value for 10 years, then return the £100 to the bondholder. The 5% yield is known as the nominal yield, or the coupon.

You will now understand why a bond, too, is a nominal asset. If you buy at issuance at £100 and retain it for 10 years you will get £100 back, no more, no less under normal circumstances. The value has not changed. However, you will also have received interest of £50 (10 payments of £5 per annum) giving a total return of £150. At first sight this looks like a real return after inflation; however, that is a bit of an illusion because inflation is compound whilst the return on the bond is simple.

However, the bond story gets a bit more complicated because there is a secondary market in bonds of all types, and it may be possible to buy or sell the nominal £100 bond for a price that is more or less than face value.

Indeed, the price of a bond could well drop immediately after launch. In our example above, let's say the price falls to £90 for a £100 nominal holding. You still get your £5 interest on the bond, although the yield has now changed from 5% to 6% (£5 / £90 times 100 – as prices rise, yields fall and vice versa), and if you hold it to redemption you will still get your £100 back (all being well).

So there is scope for realising gains on bonds and although bonds do sometimes trade above their face value the upside is limited.

The value at which the bond trades in the secondary market is affected by a number of factors. These may be external (systemic) or internal (non-systemic). Systemic factors include the general level of interest rates. If these rise or fall, then bond yields will do likewise to maintain some connection to general interest rates, within the context of risk in the bond. Non-systemic factors include the performance of the issuing government, authority or company. If this deteriorates, investors will sell their bond holdings, the price will drop and the yield will rise. We see here a direct correlation between risk and yield; in fact, some bonds are so risky, and their yields so high, that they are technically termed non-investment grade bonds or junk bonds. It is possible to lose the entire value of the bond in the event that the company or institution goes into liquidation. However, bonds rank higher in the pecking order than shares, though below bank debt and any taxes owed.

Sometimes bonds are so popular their price rises well in excess of face value and yields drop to the point where there seems no point in buying them. We saw this in the US and UK sovereign debt markets in the period 2010 to 2012. The reason is that US treasuries and UK gilts were seen as a safe haven in a very risk-averse world. At least your money is safe here, even if it does not earn anything.

Duration is also important when looking at bonds. The yield curve plots interest rates against duration. In normal circumstances the curve rises with duration. In other words, the longer the time you relinquish the right to your cash, the higher the price you ask for the privilege. However, market forces occasionally conspire to reverse the yield curve so short-term rates end up higher than longer term rates.

---

**Essential personal finance**: fixed interest investments (bonds) exhibit volatility, albeit in a limited fashion. The capital upside is limited and the yield is also usually somewhat higher than that available from cash. There is a strong relationship between bond prices, yields, risk and interest rates.

---

**Equities** are the other side of the coin of corporate financing. The company sells a share in the company to investors. If you own shares in a company, you actually own a part of the company and you are entitled to vote at shareholder meetings. In return for investing in the company in this way, the company will try to ensure you are rewarded in two ways – growth in the capital value of your share of the company and dividends.

As the value of the company rises, so does the value of the share (at least in theory) and within the realms of reason there is no limit to the upside. However, if the company fails you would be unlikely to get anything back as a shareholder.

Unfortunately share price is the main factor on which shares are judged. However, dividends are arguably more important.

---

**Essential personal finance**: a good company will provide a consistent and rising stream of dividends, and this is what underpins the share price.

---

We also expect the directors and managers of the company to achieve above inflation growth in earnings year on year (although not always achievable, especially in a difficult economic climate). However, if this happens consistently then both the share price and the dividend will rise by more than inflation each year. This is why shares are real assets rather than nominal assets. They should achieve, over the medium to longer term, a real increase in value and income.

It is useful to think in terms of the total return on a share. This should be made up of a combination of inflation, real growth and dividends. So if inflation is 2.5% pa, the dividend yield is 2% pa and real economic growth is 3% pa then we can expect, over the medium to longer term, a total return of 7.5% pa, a not unrealistic figure under normal economic conditions.

You will note that I have been slightly hedging my bets in my description of equities, using phrases such as 'over the medium to longer term' and 'under normal economic conditions'. I could be even more dramatic and repeat the Financial Conduct Authority's standard risk warnings: the price of a share can go down as well as up and you could lose your entire investment. If you go back to the start, I talked about risk, and highlighted the volatility risk of a share portfolio. And this is the whole point about shares; they are a risk investment, their price and dividends can go down as well as up and indeed you could lose the entire amount. However, in general we would expect to see real growth of both capital and income over the medium to longer term, which is what makes them attractive.

You can hold shares in two ways, as a short-term trader or as a long-term investor; my preference, as we will see shortly, is for the long-term approach. Shares are a long-term investment. Period.

**Essential personal finance**: although shares are volatile, they have the potential to provide real gains in value and income over the medium to longer term, which makes them a key weapon in the fight against inflation.

**Alternative investments** comprise a range of investments from private equity, through commodities to hedge funds and structured products. Often viewed as the bad boys of the investment world because of their perceived high risk profiles, spectacular failures and high charges, they are becoming more important in day-to-day investment management as a means of adding diversification, reducing risk and adding stability to a portfolio.

This book is not a technical treatise on investment; instead, I want to concentrate on the planning issues. There are more than enough books available on the subject of investment management if you want to pursue this further and it is worth exploring key investment theories such as Modern Portfolio Theory (MPT), the Capital Asset Pricing Model (CAPM) and behavioural economics.

**Essential personal finance**: MPT tells us that as risk increases so does return – up to a point, after which increasing the risk in a portfolio produces only a marginal increase in return and in fact only increases the chance of a total loss of the investment.

I hope you now have a basic understanding of the main asset classes – cash, fixed interest, equities and alternatives. It now only remains to draw them together into a model that can utilise the strengths of each to deal with the key investment risks we discussed at the beginning of this chapter.

This model is called **the cascade**. It has been around in one form or another for some time, although I would not say it is in widespread use. It is difficult to say who first developed the concept, though I recall being introduced to it by the late Tony Sheppard, an early financial planner and a founder member and one time President of the Institute of Financial Planning. I understand that some of Sheppard's original planner colleagues such as Mike Hague also had some input into the model, and indeed I know that these and other planners uses a variation on this model.

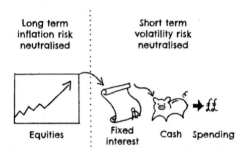

**A financial framework for neutralising risk**

The model requires you to split your portfolio into short-, medium- and longer-term tranches. The size of the smaller tranches depends, primarily, on your drawing requirements. By holding four years of drawing requirements in cash, and a further three in fixed interest / low risk assets, sufficient funds remain available to fund drawings for seven years, irrespective of stock market volatility. The balance of your assets are held in equities, where they can remain for at least seven years because you know, from your spending plans, that they are not required during that period. This tranche should, over time, become the largest element of the model. It is the part that will become the foundation of your financial security and protection from inflation over the longer term.

It is very important to emphasise that your spending plans and cash flow projections are the driving force here, and therefore ultimately your goals. Your drawing requirements are the prime determinate of the size of the tranches, rather than your views on markets, your attitude to risk or anything else. It is why you spent so much time and energy on developing current and future cash flows.

However, you may well be in a position where your income exceeds your expenses and you have a surplus. In fact, I would go further and take you back to the work we did on savings and emphasise again that you should be saving whilst you are earning. So what happens to the low risk tranches? Are they still needed? The answer is, yes, they are because at any time, although you may well be saving, there will undoubtedly be years in the not too distant future when you will need to pay for major items over and above normal cash flow, such as a replacement car, a long-haul holiday, work to your house, a wedding... If you plan on such expenditures within the short to medium term, the money should be in the lower risk tranches of your portfolio, where they are protected from stock market volatility.

Whilst you are in savings mode you can feed money into the pots. As long as you are satisfied that you have sufficient funds in the short and medium-term tranches, savings can go straight into the longer-term tranche where it can develop into the lifetime security portfolio. The model is dynamic. If you withdraw money from the short-term cash tranche, you can top it up from interest or gains from the medium- and longer-term tranches, or by directing savings, temporarily, back into the short-term tranche.

As you start to move out of work and earned income reduces, drawings will increase and the shape of the model changes somewhat. There is no investment back into the pots, and the size of the short and medium term tranches will become a little larger, reflecting the increased drawings in life with negative cash flow.

The model is highly flexible, especially if held in a modern wrap or consolidation account, and can be adjusted with reasonable ease to fit changing circumstances, which is why you should link your own variation on this financial framework with your lifetime cash flow.

The key points to note, though, are these:

> Expenditure and drawing requirements (and ultimately your goals) drive the shape of the model
> Cash should be retained where it is easily accessible, to deal with unforeseen expenditures and erratic income
> Capital for planned drawings within around seven years should be held in the short- or medium-term tranches
> As much as possible should be held in real assets in the long-term tranche, where it forms the core of your long-term financial security strategy

**Essential personal finance**: people often ask me if they can afford to take the risk of investing in equities. Given the twin perils of inflation and longevity, the question should be whether you can afford *not* to be in equities. The cascade deals with the risk in equity investment.

## HAVING THE RIGHT MONEY IN THE RIGHT PLACE AT THE RIGHT TIME

If you can get all of this right (and admittedly in this volatile, project-driven, erratic world it takes a bit of work), the benefits are invaluable. You become financially proficient, with a logical structure to your finances, driven by your expenditure plans and the achievement of your goals. You should find you always have the right money in the right place at the right time, and you will be less at the mercy of either stock market volatility or inflation.

### POSTSCRIPT

Start to make it all happen by looking at your current financial structure. Draw it as a flow chart.

Consider what needs to happen to bring about the structure I have described. Draw up a plan to make the changes, including timelines and priorities.

> - Start with your expenditure. Develop a spending plan, which will tell you how much of your income needs to be moved to your spending account each month.
> - Next, create a security fund. You may already have cash. This may be too little or too much. If too little, start to move a proportion of your income into the security fund each month until you are at least comfortable, even if you have not got the full fund in place. Excess cash can be moved to the medium or long-term tranche.
> - Address debt. Repay the most expensive debt first, then deal with less expensive debt.
> - Finally, start to build up the short-, medium- and long-term tranches.

Although I have set out the steps chronologically, it is more a question of allocation. You don't need to finish one step before moving onto the next. Think in terms of allocating income according to priorities. If, for instance, you have some immediate cash, high debts and a generous company pension scheme, you might consider allocating 30% of surplus income to a security fund, 60% to debt reduction and 10% to long-term investment. As debt reduces you might consider changing the allocations to 10%, 40% and 50%.

Try to use debit cards rather than credit cards. If you use credit cards, stick within spending plans. Repay the full amount on the card each month.

Remember that one advantage of using cards is that they provide you with a good record of your spending. It easier to track purchases paid for electronically than it is to track cash payments.

# Eight

# THE REAL MEANING OF WEALTH

'Life is a process of becoming, a combination of states we have to go through. Where people fail is that they wish to elect a state and remain in it. This is a kind of death.'

ANAÏS NIN

At the beginning of this book I listed some of the main reasons why we should take time to plan our lives and finances. These ranged from the purely practical (becoming financially proficient) to the more personal (achieving goals and freedom). However, achieving personal growth and transformation is, in my view, becoming the most important reason for financial planning. Complementary to this is a growing awareness that property is not the be all and end all; in fact, it is beginning to be seen as a gilded cage and I detect the first stirrings of a property backlash. In this chapter I want to expand on these themes and spend some time discussing how financial life planning can help to bring about personal growth and development through a reduction in exposure to property and an increase in the travel budget, and introduce the concept of real wealth being measured in terms of personal ability, spirituality and integrity.

Personal development and growth is becoming a more common objective amongst financial life planning clients. We often talk about how financial life planning is about achieving goals, and indeed that is what it is usually advertised as. I believe, however, that the true goal of personal financial life planning is to achieve personal growth. If you look at the list of common goals set out in the chapter on self-exploration you will see that they all involve a degree of self-development, whether the goal be around having a better relationship with your spouse or partner, achieving greater personal integrity, education and creativity or helping in your local community.

Staying still is not an option. If we do that we simply fall by the wayside. Growth usually requires a journey, often a journey into a part of ourselves, or the world, that we have not been to before. There is an element of the journey in growing. To this end I see a trend towards financial planning being about providing the resources to grow, usually through education and travel and specifically transformative travel or travel with a purpose.

Up to now travel has usually sat somewhere towards the end of the expenses column of a financial plan, a figure attached to it and holidays taken with that budget. It is my contention that that expenditure item should be given far higher prominence, renamed Personal Development, put at the top of the priority list after savings and used for travel for transformation, whether that be to visit friends and relatives, to educate yourself, to explore yourself or your fellow human beings, their history, their culture, their lives, to teach or care for others, to explore, to be adventurous.

It is necessary to travel to grow – not necessarily to travel to somewhere, just to travel away from somewhere: our home. We have many ways of describing our home:

> - My home is my castle
> - Home is where the heart is
> - Home is where my friends are

These may well be valid descriptions, emphasising the safe haven nature of the home. Whilst we bring up our children we need that safe haven, and in time, if we are not careful, it can become a cage, and in many cases after a huge investment of money, a gilded cage at that.

So what is the bottom line in shifting the emphasis of our planning from property ownership to transformative travel? Primarily it will bring about greater personal integrity and we should feel more comfortable in our own skins. Alain de Botton writes in his book *The Art of Travel*[27] that 'the domestic setting keeps us tethered to the person we are in ordinary life, who may not be who we essentially are'.

De Botton is saying that we entrap ourselves in a false life through an overemphasis on the home. As a financial planner I concur with his view, seeing the home as a gilded cage that locks up capital, reduces liquidity, becomes a haven from which we find it difficult to escape and prevents us achieving our true potential as human beings, hence the dichotomy between the ordinary person and the essential person. Shifting the emphasis from property ownership to personal development through transformative travel brings about a convergence between the ordinary me and the essential me, and a consequent increase in personal integrity.

Because we have greater personal integrity we should see less stress in our lives, or rather stress in a different form. Much of the stress we suffer today is the stress that arises from not being true to ourselves, for living an ordinary life rather than an essential life. As we take steps to develop and grow this stress will grow and be replaced by the stress of challenging ourselves to take those transformative journeys. Every time we move out of the gilded cage

---

[27] De Botton, Alain, *The Art of Travel*, Penguin 2002

of our domestic environment, and into a new world we will challenge ourselves, almost as if we were going through a new initiation ceremony. In her book *A Short History of Myth*, Karen Armstrong describes how initiation ceremonies in traditional tribal societies subject initiates to intense stress as they are taken from the secure domestic environment in which the initiate dies to his old (childhood) self and is reborn as a man. Facing up to the trauma helps him to understand that death is a new beginning. It is 'a rite of passage to a new form of existence'[28].

Importantly, Armstrong emphasises that this happens every time we leave the comfort and security of our home and go through the trauma and stress of a transformative journey. Each time, we die to our old self and are reborn to a new self. The more we do this, the more we are able to see death as simply 'the last and final initiation into another, totally unknown mode of being'.

Our own personal, daily initiation ceremonies do not have to be the same as those of traditional societies, which we might perceive as being unnecessarily brutal. Interestingly, Armstrong talks about how a novel, 'if it is written and read with serious attention, can help us to make a painful rite of passage from one phase of life, one state of mind, to another'.

By shifting the emphasis of our plans to personal development we should see a huge increase in our self-worth. We will break out of our own personal prisons, become less reliant on others (always a drain on our energy and self-worth) and become world changers. Through personal growth and transformation we stop being part of the problem and become part of the solution, and in so doing enhance our own respect for our self, and our worth in the eyes of others.

---

[28] Armstrong, Karen. *A Short History of Myth*. Cannongate, 2005

**Essential personal finance**: personal wealth is greatly enhanced by abandoning the illusory wealth of property and replacing it with the far greater wealth of a developed, world-changing human being.

A home is important. In particular it is an important shelter for growing children, a place of warmth, comfort and security and I am not suggesting we should abandon our shelters for yurts or tepees as an alternative place in which to raise our families, although it is not unheard of. However, once the children have left home it is important to re-assess our relationship with property, which in the UK is now bordering on an obsession, an obsession fuelled by money.

Over the last 50 or 60 years we have monetised property. Far less is it seen as a home, something personal and domestic; instead our first thoughts about a property these days tend to be about what it is worth. Property has changed from a used asset to a financial asset.

The advent of easy mortgages, and very easy mortgages in the last decade, has also helped to monetise property through leverage. For a while, it was possible to obtain mortgages of 100% of the value of the property. As a buyer you could acquire a house without putting in a penny of your own money. In a rising market, the principle of leverage ensured fabulous profits for very little initial investment.

To be fair, 100% mortgages were not the norm and home-buyers did have to put in their own money. A common scenario is homeowners expending most of their capital on the home, either in the form of equity on initial purchase, or on expenditure to improve the property, turning it into their dream home. As a result, they end up asset rich, cash poor. Indeed, many of those who came to me and other financial planners in the 2000s were in that position, a situation often compounded by excessive debt.

It is not even a recent phenomenon. I recall being asked for advice by a couple in Leeds in the late 80s. On this occasion I visited them in their home. They had retired a year or so earlier and built their dream house, and the first half hour of our meeting was spent on a conducted tour of the property, which they gave with huge pride, showing me all the bells and whistles of their dream home. When we turned to finances and I asked what the problem was they told me they seemed a little bit short of cash. An exploration of their finances proved that to be an understatement. They had no capital left at all, and their pension income barely covered their basic outgoings. Truly they had built a gilded cage for themselves, leaving them with the realisation that they would have to sell to raise capital and reduce costs if they wanted to live any sort of fulfilled life in their retirement.

Today our society is obsessed with property in a way our parents never were. We spend fortunes on the most expensive fittings and fixtures when actually a kitchen is a kitchen is a kitchen as long as it works. Whilst I am not advocating that we should live in nothing more than a stone tent or a monk's cell, I suggest we have got the balance between life and property a bit about face at the moment.

It is important to understand, as the Leeds couple began to, that there is an opportunity cost to property, and that cost, to put it simply, is liquidity, which translates into the ability to *do* and ultimately to grow into the true me. If we return to George Kinder's concept of 'money maturity', we can view excessive investment in our homes and property as immature as it keeps us in the childhood *getting* phase of our lives, holding us back from the more important doing and being. We entrap ourselves in our property, electing a state as Nin puts it, and remaining in it in a form of death.

This is a shame, because there is no escaping our real death, after which our property is going to be of no use to us.

For much of the past two decades property has been a main source of funding our lifestyle. As prices rose and equity grew, we simply re-mortgaged. Our property became our friendly bank manager and funded a lifestyle way beyond what our income would allow. This too helped to create an obsession with property, aided and abetted by banks and building societies eager to lend more money. This money started to come from wholesale sources rather than high street savers and this sowed the seeds of the 2008 financial crises, the after effects of which are still with us and will be for many years.

Although a sense of perspective seems to be returning to the property market, it is being forced on householders by circumstances. The change does not yet really come from the heart, although I do now advise a small number of clients who have elected to abandon property ownership and rent instead, a course that allows them a very different lifestyle.

Let's turn to the other side of the equation, personal growth and development. If you are reading this book, you are almost certainly a person for whom standing still is anathema. You almost certainly want to change the world or leave your mark on the world in some way. In order to do that you will want to grow your skills, gain a greater outlook on the world, explore way beyond your immediate environment, discover yourself.

As nearly all my clients tell me, moving beyond their comfort zone is important. I call this travel with a purpose or transformative travel. The word 'travel' probably over romanticises the journey, which could simply involve attending a short course at a local adult education centre. However, there are two elements to this. The first is the **journey**, the physical act of moving out of the comfort zone of the home or day-to-day work environment. Any such journey into a new environment is, as Karen Armstrong puts it, an initiation, a challenge and self-induced stress that changes us. We die to our old self, even if it is in a small way, and are reborn anew, every time we challenge ourselves by moving into a new environment.

The second part is the **destination** (although that too may still be a journey), where we start to explore new ideas (or even old ideas), visit new people, see different ways of life and generally find a new perspective on the world. Our destination may be professional, in the form of any number of retreats or programmes available on the market today. Whilst some of these simply impart knowledge, the really valuable programmes (and the most expensive) are those that help you to change, to transform, to implement some new model or process or vision.

We may want to travel to discover other cultures, contemporary or ancient, from which we can learn new perspectives. We may want to travel to visit relatives and friends, and since family and friends are often at the top of the list of life goals this is important. Indeed, one of the real issues that the couple from Leeds had was that they could not even raise the money to visit their daughter in Australia.

We may want to use our professional skills to help others in near or far parts of the world. In helping others in different environments we probably learn as much about ourselves as we give to those we are helping. One of my clients, a recently-retired doctor, now travels frequently to Southern Africa, using his skills to bring comfort and healing to others. At the same time he too grows.

I certainly believe the best result of this strategy is to gain a degree of personal integrity and spirituality that is missing from most of us at the moment. By demoting property and possessions in our order of priorities we create space to listen to ourselves and discover who we really are and what we can really do. Spirituality is a right brain activity and allowing room for our spirit helps to overcome the increasing dominance of the left brain, especially in matters financial.

There are many, many examples of transformative travel, too many to list. However, all we are doing is enhancing the natural progression of life. We start adult life in *having* mode, then move into *doing* mode before finally entering *being* mode, where we actually start to live. Downgrading property in our lives and using released capital and income to fund transformative travel accelerates the process. We cannot take our property and possessions with us to the grave, so why wait till the last minute to abandon them? At the same time our travelling helps us to find ourselves, to become our true selves living with integrity. It also prepares us for death, which simply becomes the last in a series of transformative initiation ceremonies in which we die to our old self and are reborn to our new self, as Karen Armstrong puts it.

That is the theory, so how does it work in practice. I have already presented a case study of over-investment in property and I mentioned a few of my clients who have elected to rent rather than buy property. One individual in particular has taken the concept to heart. After selling his house five years ago he elected to rent and has found a reasonable property with a good landlord who looks after the property. My client runs his own consultancy business and has set limits on the amount of time he will work, using the rest of his time for travel with a purpose by attending courses, travelling to explore new parts of the world and cultures and learning about himself and others. His capital is invested and under our guidance he uses it in a controlled way to fund his travelling.

This is a classic example of how financial life planning can truly help you to achieve amazing goals. Obviously a life strategy that seeks to reduce your reliance on and tether to property and replace it with an agenda of travel and personal development has huge financial implications. Nonetheless, in attempting to make this change, the normal life financial planning process will apply. Indeed, running with the process is a sure way of achieving the change. As usual, you need to look at where you are now and build a starting point. Next comes the process of developing your goals in detail; what do you really want to achieve, what are your weaknesses, and where do you want to develop, and in what direction?

With clear goals in place you can start to build spending and cash flow plans using your lifetime cash flow, pricing in any travel or projects you have included in your plans. This is the important bit, and is the place where life and money meet. You have set out what you want from life, and the spending plans and cash flow model enable you to put in place an architecture for your finances that will support your goals.

Then comes dealing with the obstacles, of which the main is transitioning from a large to a smaller house, or selling your home and exchanging it for a rental property. With your newly released capital, financial planning, cash flow planning in particular, will help you work out how you should invest the capital in a way that enables you to use it to further your goals whilst ensuring you don't run out of money before you die.

The other issue you will have to deal with here is your role as the filling in the sandwich between the bread of the older and younger generations in your life. Although your children are probably leaving school and even university, and becoming independent, they will want and need your care and help for a while yet. This will involve finding the time to give them the love and support they will need, and that you will want to give, and it may also include financial support such as help with buying their own home or higher education.

As your children become older, more independent and less of a call on your emotional and financial resources, your parents are probably doing the reverse, and although they will have probably said to you many times in the past that they don't want to be a burden on you in their old age, that is what they will become. Once again, whether from a sense of duty, or from a deep love of your parents, you will be there for them.

Hopefully, if they have been financially savvy they will not be a financial burden. Rather, in their old age, they will need physical and emotional support and it's going to fall on your shoulders to provide it. Even if they are in good health and active at the moment, it is important that you discuss with them, in practical, serious terms, how they want to live and be treated as they grow old, and what role you may want to have in their lives. As much of their wealth may be in their property, and be required for their old age, you might want to pool resources and have one single family house, particularly if one of your parents has already died leaving the other on his or her own. Alternatively, you might feel it is important to live close to your parents where you can keep an eye on them. All these things need to be considered and planned for. Doing so will leave you in a better position to achieve your own goals.

## HARNESSING THE POWER OF MONEY

Good cash flow planning will help you understand how much you need to draw from your enhanced investment portfolio each year in the furtherance of your important personal projects and development plans. It will enable you to develop an asset allocation plan, holding cash in reserve to cover short-term drawings, then holding assets in a low risk portfolio to cover medium term drawings. This will give you the security of being able to invest the bulk of your portfolio in real assets such as shares and property and alternatives to secure your lifetime security and protect you from inflation. The review process (of which more in Chapter 10) is also important and will enable you to monitor the progress of your projects and finances.

These are radical ideas and can lead to a transformation in your lives and an enhanced, more spiritual life where you can live with integrity and achieve things you may not have otherwise been able to do.

### POSTSCRIPT

At the end of Chapter 5 I encouraged you not to forget about yourself by developing your own mind, body and spirit plan to keep you in good mental, physical and spiritual health.

The next stage is to build this into your own personal development plan. This will be formed primarily by your goals. A lack of skills may be a major obstacle to achieving some of your goals. For instance, you have always had an interest in Italian history, culture and art and want to explore further; to achieve this, you might decide it is necessary to learn Italian. You want to complete John Cleare's 10 great treks of the world, so your personal development plan may include getting walking fit, honing your trekking and camping skills, and researching the countries into which you will be travelling. You yearn for a more spiritual life, so you might attend a retreat or meditation course.

Whatever it is you need, put it into your plans and cost it out.

# Nine

# FINANCIAL WISDOM AND POWER FROM PATIENCE

'Everything begins and ends at exactly
the right time and place.'

JOAN LINDSAY, AUTHOR OF *PICNIC AT HANGING ROCK*

Patience is probably not a buzzword of the modern world. Nor would one normally associate it with money. However, we have already seen how patience, in conjunction with compounding, brings significant rewards. In the world of financial life planning, patience goes somewhat further than the simple mathematics of time and rolled-up returns. It is less about time, more about timing, choosing the right time to do nothing and the right time to act. It is not procrastination; it is being fully present in the moment and preparing yourself to be in the right time and place, armed with the right knowledge and principles, to begin and end something at exactly the right time and place. And it is about having the right money in the right place at the right time to live your desired life for all your life.

Time and patience may seem to be in conflict. Time, after all, is limited and the longer we live the scarcer a resource it becomes. Patience, on the other hand, requires us to sit back and do nothing. Patience, if you want, is Dante's dark wood again, taking the long route to wisdom rather than the shortcut to immediate gratification. The urge, especially in the fast moving world in which we live and work, is to do it, do it, do it whilst we have time.

**Essential personal finance:** Sitting down and not doing it, the opposite of what we think we should be doing, can be immensely rewarding.

" I'M SITTING DOWN AND NOT DOING IT ! "

If time is so scarce, why is patience so important? Well, patience is the key to understanding and ultimately to wisdom. Tolstoy talked about time and patience being 'the two most powerful warriors', and St Augustine called patience 'the companion of wisdom'. Patience is the key to understanding, which George Kinder, the father of financial life planning, sees as the central and most important of his *Seven Stages of Money Maturity*. As early as the 5th century BC the link between patience and understanding was recognised by Lao-tzu, a philosopher from ancient China, who asked 'Do you have the patience to wait till your mud settles and the water is clear?'

In today's go faster culture the question is even more relevant because patience is about planning your money rather than rushing headlong into the next purchase. Patience allows the mud of our lives and environment to clear and enables us to understand our relationship to money, and with that understanding comes growth and transformation.

Time and patience, of course, are the most important elements of investment, as we discovered in the chapter on compound interest. Time is the ingredient that underpins the accumulation of wealth through monthly savings and compound returns. Patience is the key to long-term investment performance.

---

**Essential personal finance:** the investor who spends time planning his or her investments then waits has a greater chance of successful outcomes than the impatient investor who cannot live with investment losses, is always chasing the next best investment idea and dealing daily in the hope of a quick buck.

---

Investment is like fine wine; both need time and patience to mature and come to their true potential. Trying to hasten the process of fermentation and settling or initial investment selection and compound returns tends to end in disaster. The wonderful adverts for Jack Daniels, which went entirely against the grain of modern life by showing shots of elderly gentlemen sitting around the distillery whittling sticks and occasionally slouching past barrels of product paying them no attention whatsoever where entirely legitimate, and a useful lesson to both distillers and investors. To this end, investors and financial planners have much in common. In our profession, nothing needs to be rushed. Patience is the key to success, not action and activity particularly when it is simply for the sake of doing something.

I often think of my older clients in particular as being very similar to the cellar man at the distillery. We have a slow, gentle relationship; we review the situation each year at least and often decide that nothing needs to be done. The clients just carry on living the life they want to, with financial security and certainty.

Whilst the time value of money is a very left-brain, logical function, the relationship between time, patience, wisdom and understanding is more of a right brain activity, and just as important in our dealings with money, possibly even more so. I have already mentioned George Kinder's work in this area, and would say that he has nailed it. For Kinder, understanding is the key to dealing with our often painful emotions around money. Understanding, in turn, is achieved by patience. Having the patience to let the mud settle brings understanding as the water clears. In turn, understanding allows wisdom to grow in us, and so wisdom around money comes from dealing with our painful emotions around money, through patience and understanding.

The financial life planning movement, due in the main to George Kinder's leadership, has embraced meditation as a way of turning pain around money into wisdom. Kinder is passionate about meditation and his book *Transforming Suffering Into Wisdom: The Art of Inner Listening* is an excellent treatise on the subject and will be of help to beginners and regular practitioners. His mantra here is the concept of 'Let the thoughts go, let the feelings be'. In meditation, Kinder tells us, we should let go of the stories that are hooked into our feelings, and just feel the feelings, the emotions swirling around our body. Just being with our feelings, which contain huge energy and power, can bring a real sense of calm, perspective and understanding.

I know from experience that meditation can produce surprisingly positive results. Possibly one of the most stunning examples occurred when I tried to park my car to avoid putting money in the meter one morning when I was in a hurry and had to stop briefly at the office before driving to a meeting. The usual free slots in the town were already full, I didn't want to 'waste' an hour's parking for 10 minutes, so I parked rather badly in a local shop owner's slot. When I got back to the car my car was boxed in, and I was angry with the owner and myself, especially as I was running late. I hunted round, found the car owner and brusquely asked him to move the car, incurring some comments about people parking their cars properly in the town, a comment which angered me even more because I am normally scrupulous about this, parking tidily to allow as much room as possible for others in our town's limited car parking spaces.

Having got clear, I shot off thinking only of what had just happened, very rankled about it and all just to try to save a pound in the meter. I had driven about two miles before I suddenly realised I was completely unaware of the here and now. My thoughts about the incident had been so intrusive they had taken over, leaving me driving on instinct. The pain of the humiliation and the anger at being late had completely taken over, a dangerous situation that, fortunately, had not resulted in any accidents. So I stopped in a lay-by and sat in the car meditating, letting my thoughts, the story, go and just feeling my anger in its almost physical form, just to be with it, to nurse it and accept it without thinking about the story.

The result was that, within minutes, I had returned to the here and now, calm had been restored and most importantly, a solution had presented itself. I was able to be fully present for the rest of the day at my meetings and events. Had I not done so, the episode would have gnawed at me all day and beyond. It would have sat there in my gut like a poisoned frog, as I clung to the story and the feelings it created in me. As it was, the short meditation defused the situation in the shortest possible time, turning a debilitating anger into a creative calmness, out of which a course of action presented itself. I decided, on my return, to seek out the owner of the other car in his shop and apologise, which he accepted gracefully and which developed into a conversation about the town's parking facilities and the council's parking charges. Patience, meditation, understanding, wisdom, power.

So meditation does help. It helps to bring calm and perspective, especially in matters surrounding money. It helps you to really be present, living in the moment, the here and now and not in the past regretting what we have done or in the future, fearing what may happen. It is a form of emptying, kenosis, leaving your mind clear of distracting stories and thoughts, providing the blank sheet of paper that I advocated in my second chapter.

If you have not meditated before there are many resources to help you. I have already mentioned Kinder's book and there are many more on the market.

## STEP BY STEP TO CLEAR WATER

**Meditation:** join a local meditation group or start with a guided meditation at home.

Meditation Oasis is a website that offers a number of downloadable meditations by Mary Maddux, including a four-week beginners' course in meditation. Her Stress Relief meditation, which echoes Kinder's thoughts and feelings mantra to perfection, is invaluable. And I have already mentioned my favourite meditative practice of walking.

Living in the moment is an important part of financial life planning. Often we spend time thinking about the past, the mistakes we have made and the regrets about things we didn't do, and in particular our experiences with money, both good and bad. Whilst the past has valuable lessons for us, dwelling in the past is probably not very healthy. In spite of its ups and downs, the past offers a place of security and certainty, because it has actually happened. However, it is a form of clinging. As Blake would say, binding oneself to the past is a sure way of destroying the 'winged life', and prevents us 'living in eternity's sunrise'. The past is all about our stories and thoughts, and meditation is a great way of moving from the past to the present.

**Essential personal finance**: meditation is a practice which brings us to the here and now, living for the real moment and not the past.

Alternatively, we spend time in the future, the unknown, seen by some as a place of uncertainty and fear, and by others as a place of opportunity and future riches. As we need to be aware of the past and learn its lessons, so we need to plan for the future, which is what this whole book is about, indeed what financial life planning is about. Financial life planning enables us to deal with the uncertainties of the future, to identify opportunities and put in place action plans to take advantage of them. In so doing we lose our fear of the future and our greed for its opportunities and potential rewards. With a good life plan we are able to stop thinking about the future and are more able to live in the present.

## THE MOST VALUABLE TIME OF OUR LIVES

So what does the present have to offer? The answer lies, possibly, with the butterfly,

> 'who counts not months but moments,
> and has time enough'
>
> RABINDRANATH TAGORE

In the present we have died to our old selves, and not yet been born to our future selves and so it is the most valuable time of our lives. This moment is the only time in our lives in which we are truly alive, a valuable moment if ever there was one and one not to be cluttered with fears of the future or regrets for the past. Surprising though it may seem, financial life planning helps you to live in the present moment, and in partnership with regular meditation is an invaluable aid to a fulfilled life.

## POSTSCRIPT

It seems that meditation can also benefit your health, a nice added bonus. Early research was undoubtedly flawed because of poor research methodologies and the absence of randomised control trials to eliminate the placebo effect. However, recent and more methodical research making use of non-invasive technology such as fMRI and EEG are beginning to show some measurable, positive health benefits. These are often to do with stress and pain reduction, which in turn have a benefit on the cardiovascular and nervous systems.

Of the four main meditation schools (mantra, mindfulness, yoga and T'ai Chi / Qigong), mindfulness does lay serious claim to stress reduction benefits, with some businesses and hospitals openly advocating its use. However, whilst some evidence shows it can help with the relief of symptoms and improve lifestyle quality, there is little, if any, firm evidence to show that it can prevent or cure disease.

In spite of this, the Mindfulness Based Stress Reduction programme (MBSR) developed by Jon Kabat-Zinn and delivered here in the UK by practitioners such as Jane Brendgan are popular and effective.

Mindfulness is defined by Kabat-Zinn as 'moment-to-moment, non-judgemental awareness', a definition that explains why it complements the form of financial life planning I advocate in this book. Both enable us to live in the moment without regrets for the past and fear of the future. Both promote non-judgemental compassion (for both for self and others) over egotism, which is closely associated with money.

If you want to explore this further, then I would suggest *The Miracle of Mindfulness* by Buddhist monk and Nobel Peace Prize nominee Thich Nhat Hanh is a good place to start.

## Ten

# RENEWING YOUR PLAN

'Change and renewal are themes in life, aren't they? We keep growing throughout life.'

SUSAN MINOT

R enewal is important; it is also the one element of the planning process that has tended to be put on the back burner, both by financial advisers and individuals.

It is important because plans rarely survive contact with reality. This is especially the case if you are a freeforming entrepreneur with a family, a situation that leaves you vulnerable to events in many different quarters of your life. You might ask, therefore, why you should even plan at all. As I pointed out earlier, it's the process as much as the plan itself that is important. In addition, you yourself will know that there is a much better chance of success with a plan than without one.

Events engage us all the time, from the minor to the significant. Some are distressing, others joyful.

**Essential personal finance**: events all fall into one of two categories, those we can control and those we cannot.

The renewal process is a way of helping us to deal with those events we cannot control, particularly the macro-economic events that shape our plans. The renewal process should help us to adjust everything in our financial plan from asset allocation to debt levels and expenditure to take account of those events we cannot control. Events we can control, of course, are part of the plan itself.

Our goals may change. This may be for any number of reasons. As we grow older and more experienced, we may start to revalue what is important in our lives and hence see the need to ditch original goals in favour of new goals. Events such as the arrival of children or the death of our parents will put a new perspective on life. And of course, as you go through life you will actually achieve some of your goals, at which point you might decide that is enough, I've done it, now I can relax and settle. It's more likely, though, that being who you are you will simply up the ante and replace your achieved goal with a new, more challenging goal. I ran a half marathon in under two and a quarter hours, so next time I will aim for under two hours.

However, it is not usually this clear cut, especially when it comes to families. You and your partner may decide you want to have two children, and with two boys you decide to go for a third for a girl. Children give rise to a huge range of changing aspirations, particularly around where and how to bring them up, where to educate them, how to split time between family and work. And until they arrive, you just don't know what you are in for. When you join that elite club of people who are parents you join a new world, one that keeps you on your toes for twenty to thirty years and has an enormous impact on your life.

One friend of mine, a single mum living in London, was thrilled with the primary state education her son received in London whilst nursing deep concerns about the secondary education available. Her son was a bright, outgoing boy and she wanted the best education for him. Having visited us and talked to our friends in Yorkshire, she made the brave decision to relocate to Yorkshire and enrol her son in the local secondary school, where he did very well, becoming Head Boy. For her, the financial implications and the disruption were significant, and well worthwhile.

Take care not to ditch goals or personal projects simply because they are proving more challenging to achieve than you expected. If you are not there, it is because there will be obstacles in the way and these will be a challenge. However, that does not mean you should ditch the goal, so it becomes a regret that you never got there.

> **Essential personal finance**: the renewal process should be an opportunity for you to re-evaluate the route you take to deal with obstacles in your path.

Our circumstances change and a plan that might have been suitable two or three years ago may now be out of date because our circumstances have changed significantly. Our business may have developed and grown far faster than we expected, or even vice versa. Our children may have changed, requiring a new plan. Our parents may have become less able, needing more attention from us. All of these, and many more, are good reasons why we should renew our plans at least annually.

## CHANGE AND RENEWAL

It's also important to understand that the planning process itself leads to change in our lives, and often not the change we expected. Our lives, and our plans for them, are not usually as straightforward as setting a goal, achieving it and moving on. As we change, and our lives change, we need to renew our plans constantly.

This is the principle of equifinality, an important concept that needs to be taken into account always. Usually referred to in systems theory, it simply states that a given outcome or destination can be reached through many different means or routes. So in moving from your present situation, Point A, to a desired situation, Point D, you could go via Points B or C. In real life there are often many different strategies and routes to achieving your goal. The next step is to understand that the route you choose may actually lead you Point E, an entirely different destination from your plan. On your journey your experiences and events may lead you to decide that Point D is no longer appropriate, and instead you are going to aim for Point E instead. That, of course, needs a new plan.

How should we deal with our goals in the renewal process? Whilst short-term goals might be quite firm and well defined, longer term goals can be less so. In fact, it is probably more useful to express longer-term goals as a range rather than a point. In the annual renewal process, you can narrow the range as you get closer to the target. For example, if you are in your mid 40s at the moment and are thinking terms of becoming financially independent you might express this as looking to be in a position of not having to work sometime after 62 and certainly no later the 67. This is not being wishy-washy about your goals, just being realistic. Life is not a certainty, and you could be in a position to be able to stop work well before 65 if things go well, though it may be later if progress is slower.

---

**Essential personal finance**: each time you renew your plan you can narrow the range, become more precise and more certain about your goal and your ability to achieve it.

---

You might also consider the probability of success in achieving something, and look at this at the time you renew your plans. Financial planners often use Monte Carlo simulations to assess the probability of achieving specific objectives, usually relating to the size of a portfolio at a future point in time. Monte Carlo runs a series of simulations with different variables within a given range to assess the probability of achieving a particular objective. This can be helpful in terms of assessing the realism of achieving a longer term financial objective, such as becoming independent. In the above example, for instance, a simulation may show that there is only a 70% chance, given defined parameters, of achieving sufficient funds to be independent by 62. This might be a trigger for you to either extend the time period, or at least to look at other parameters to achieve your goal. Once again, carried out annually the exercise will help to bring definition and certainty to your goals.

Recalculating your personal key financial ratios will help you to assess the degree to which you are achieving your goals, as well as checking your security. You can also compare to last year, and see if the ratios have got better or worse, or are on track, and if not, why not. Remember, though, that an above average movement in a ratio may be due to an above average movement in asset prices, which may reverse next year, so don't start making hasty decisions about your money based on just one year's movement. Take the long view here.

In planning your life and money you might want to set boundaries beyond which you absolutely will not go. This is particularly useful if you are finding it difficult to set specific objectives. For instance, returning to the earlier example, you may not want to make a decision on exactly when you want to be in a position where you have sufficient capital not to have to work if you don't want to, though you may say to yourself that you must be at that point by age 70. This at least gives you a planning position on which to work. In the shorter term, you may not know quite how you are going to spend your money because your short-term situation is a little unclear, so you might put an absolute upper limit on your expenditure this year, and leave flexibility on how you spend it.

"Darling, we are not in control of our finances!"

Another example is setting the balance between family and work. A general objective may be to spend more time with your family, and you recognise the nature of your position as a business owner means that you cannot plan this in the same way as an employed person with set hours and holiday allowances may be able to. Therefore, you might put an overall limit on your total working hours in a given time period, a boundary that you will not cross under any circumstances. You might recall in an earlier chapter I talked about financial life planning being about achieving freedom within boundaries. The annual renewal of your plan is about precisely this, achieving freedom by renewing your boundaries.

## THE RENEWAL PROCESS

Let's go into the mechanics of your plan renewal. The first question is when? You should renew your plan at least annually – on the date you decided earlier would be your renewal or planning date. However, you may want to revisit the plan at intervals between, such as half yearly or quarterly.

You should review specific elements more frequently, to ensure you are on track. The obvious example here is your expenditure of time and money, which you should look at and compare to your time and money spending plans at least weekly. Another example concerns personal tax allowances. If your personal financial year ends in August you should carry out a mini review in the run up to the end of the national tax year (5th April in the UK) to ensure you have taken up your annual allowances into pensions and other tax privileged investments you hold with limited contribution allowances. Taking up capital gains tax allowances is also a good strategy at this time of year; it's surprising how much of your free assets portfolio you can rebase in a single year without paying Capital Gains Tax (CGT) even in years of good growth. Even in poor years you might want to sell and repurchase to create losses, which can be carried forwards if permitted (though beware of over churning and the impact on performance of the costs of this exercise).

In the UK the end of the fiscal year often falls around Easter week, so give yourself plenty of time to make changes bearing in mind that many financial institutions may be closed or will have set early deadlines.

Some elements of the plan may need to be reviewed on events rather than to a specific schedule. In the UK the Chancellor makes two major speeches during the year, the Autumn Statement and the Budget. Both usually contain changes to the tax rules, which may affect your finances, and these events should trigger a quick review of your finances to check to see if you need to make changes. Similarly a big shift in markets, often caused by some sort of event, may warrant a review of your actual asset allocation to bring it back in line with your desired allocation, or events in your own life may warrant a change to both your actual and planned allocation. Once again, be aware here that any change may incur costs. However, rebalancing a portfolio to bring it into line with your planned allocation is the main, if not the only, reason for making changes to your portfolio, an exercise that can be carried out in conjunction with taking up CGT allowances.

The renewal process itself works in a similar way to the initial planning process. First, collect all the data you need and set it out in a way that makes it easy to read and understand. The primary data will be financial, and you should construct financial statements of assets and liabilities on your personal review date (so you will need to download or ask for valuations of your assets). You should develop statements of income and expenditure for the previous 12 months. You may want to produce a written statement of where you are in terms of your life at this point, a simple summary of where you are now, and where your circle of family, friends, acquaintances and colleagues are in relation to you. Here you could also summarise any major changes to your circumstances over the past twelve months.

Next, renew your objectives. Look at them in detail and discuss them within the family. Take into account the comments above about the renewal of your goals. Set out your new goals in writing.

Anecdotally, it appears that those who write down their goals are more likely to achieve them than those who do not.

The third stage is to take a slide rule to both your circumstances and objectives. You must analyse and make sense of the raw data you have acquired. Here are just some of the things you should recalculate or review:

> Net worth and cash flow
> Review of assets ('paint on the windows of the house starting to peel, may need attention this year or next', 'second car now beyond local repair and needs replacing' etc), including financial assets (are they still relevant, cost effective and supportive of my goals?)
> Liability repayment plans – are we on track to repay liabilities by the due date
> Insurance cover and insurance needs
> Personal key financial ratios
> Actual asset allocation and deviation from planned allocation
> Tax allowances and actual take up of allowances
> Your age, and the ages of your close family, highlighting any implications (eg my son is 17 and sits A-levels this year – more time needed to support him and help in his selection of university or gap-year activity, plus driving lessons and a car; mum is 60 this year – make sure she gets her bus pass)
> Any health issues that may need attention in the coming months
> Any business or career issues; what are my prospects for the coming months, what are my partner's prospects for the coming months, what is our combined gross and net income likely to be in the coming twelve months, and

> ‣ Given my objectives, what is my expenditure likely to be in the next 12 months – and beyond
> ‣ What does my long-term cash flow look like (a cash flow modelling programme is invaluable here) and what is the value of my liquid assets projected to be over the coming years. Importantly, do my liquid assets run out before I / we die?

By now, you have actually renewed you plan and, once again, its worth setting this out on paper, a quick summary of what you are going to do in the short, medium and longer term, and how much its going to cost. Within this plan you should set out any changes you need to make to your finances to ensure they are working to achieve your goals. This should include changes you need to make to your financial products, including your asset allocation, to ensure you have the correct financial architecture to achieve your goals.

---

**Essential personal finance**: your portfolio of financial products is there to support you in your life goals; if they don't, change them or adapt them.

---

The final part of the process is to compile an action plan of what you are going to do, and when in the next year. This should come as no surprise, since it is what you do in your business all the time. You should carry the action list across to your calendar or to-do list (*Remember the Milk* is a great for this) and in your calendar mark out time periods for the activities in your plan.

## STEP BY STEP TO CLEAR WATER

**Holidays:** if you plan to work 40 weeks in the year, and taking 12 weeks for holiday or personal development, get those in the calendar straight away, so you can plan your business activities around those away periods (and tell your clients, if appropriate).

### RENEWAL IS AS VALUABLE AS YOUR ORIGINAL PLAN

If you are rigorous and disciplined about this you will have a much greater chance of achieving your goals and find real freedom. Sometimes the review might result in no more than in-flight corrections to your course, whilst in some years it might result in a major change of direction, or the re-routing of your course to avoid obstacles on the way to your original destination and consequent changes to your finances. Either way it is the process that is of real value as much as the final plan itself.

## POSTSCRIPT

Renewal is also a good time to look in depth at our own internal needs and drives, our personal interests, and their political and financial implications.

Politics is about the allocation of resources in an environment of scarcity. In our lives we are allocated scarce resources (salaries or social security, for instance) and we allocate scarce resources in our own households (food, housing, entertainment).

Its hardly surprising, therefore, that as a species, we have evolved from *homo sapiens* to *homo politicus*.

We now, even if subconsciously, build our own political power bases in order to protect, nurture and develop our own personal interests. We need to have sufficient resources to run those power bases, to build and maintain the alliances that will advance our personal interests. Indeed, money itself is a source of power and the accumulation of power is often a key motivator for the accumulation of wealth.

However, our own personal interests usually go far beyond the accumulation of money and power, and will underpin our more overt goals.

Indeed, more important than money may be our security or our status, or the need to be loved or respected or to be recognised as a success in our field or as a competent person or world changer.

In my own case security is a key driver, a result of some fairly disastrous financial decisions when I was young. This has driven the design of my business, which is about secure cash flow and steady growth rather than risky ventures that may or may not produce the occasional big win. This in turn is reflected in our own family financial plans, although I sense that a need to make the world a better place for all who live in it is becoming a more powerful drive as I get older, and with that comes the need to take more risks.

These are deeply personal issues and ones that we don't often articulate. However much they remain out of sight, they can have a tremendous influence on the way we act, on the goals we formulate, and on the way we lead our lives.

Political man and woman some twenty years ago tended to concentrate on 'my rights', what's in it for me, rather than 'my responsibilities'. I think that has changed to one in which the political individual recognises the power of alliances and indeed that strong alliances are built on what you give to the party, not what you take.

That, surely, is something we need to build into our financial plans.

# Eleven

# MAKING LIFE AND MONEY FLOURISH

'My mission in life is not merely to survive,
but to thrive; and to do so with some passion, some
compassion, some humor, and some style.'

MAYA ANGELOU

By now you will have realised that financial life planning is not a quick fix, instant solution to happiness and financial freedom. It takes hard work and self-discipline and you may feel daunted by what I am proposing you do. Indeed, we have covered much ground in the preceding 10 chapters, in which I hope I have explained why financial life planning is so important in the context of the world in which we live today. I have asked you to look deeply inside yourself, to discover where you stand in your life and with your money. I have asked you to think deeply about the way you want to live your life and the values you wish to live by. We have looked at dealing with the obstacles that will get in your way and learnt about managing both your time and your money. I have provided you with a model for arranging your investments and I have asked you to redefine wealth away from investment in property to investment in yourself.

Financial life planning is not simply about writing a plan. It is about changing the way you deal with your life and money. It is about the journey you take and the changes you make in the process of producing your plan and it is about living your plan from day-to-day. To help you in this Herculean task I set out in this final chapter some of the fundamental tenets that underpin a good financial life plan, I summarise the six steps you can take to formulate your own plan (and change your life) and I provide a breakdown of a practical financial framework.

## FUNDAMENTAL TENETS

My personal experiences, my clients' experiences and the knowledge I have developed from personal development programmes I have attended have helped me formulate a set of values and beliefs around money and life which speak to spiritual emergence and underpin my own life and my businesses:

### Spirit of money

> Money is a means to an end, not an end in itself
> Letting go is essential to transforming your life and money
> A good financial plan will help you to live in the moment and be really present in the here and now by compensating for regrets for the past and neutralising fear of the future
> Money is a pawn of the ego. This often leads to poor or even damaging life and financial decisions. Compassion for self and others provides a better decision making environment
> True wealth comes from investment in ourselves, rather than investment in financial assets
> Taking personal responsibility for one's decisions and control of one's affairs is non-negotiable

## Goals

> You have to plan your finances to support your profound life goals, and you cannot change your life without addressing your finances

> Don't delay achieving your goals; you don't know what tomorrow might bring. There must be a balance between achieving important goals in the short term and being responsible for long-term financial security

> Usually, the most profound life goals are centred around family and friends; they can require a lot of time without costing much in financial terms

## Planning and organisation

> Plans set boundaries for your time and money; boundaries might have to be drawn tight initially and can be expanded as your life and finances become stronger

> A financial plan should help you organise your finances to ensure you always have the right money in the right place at the right time to achieve your important and profound goals as quickly and efficiently as possible

> Planned and controlled spending lies at the heart of a successful financial plan

> Plan only those things you can control; plan for those things you cannot control

> Financial peace of mind is achieved by understanding your current personal and financial situation; even if it's not good, at least you know it and can do something about it

> A financial framework and structure is the route to personal freedom

## Products and investments

> The test for whether a financial product is right for you is whether it will support or hinder you in the achievement of your life goals

> Portfolio success should be measured in terms of the achievement of your profound life goals, not by investment returns or performance relative to a benchmark

> Of the two key threats to a portfolio, short-term volatility and long-term inflation, inflation is the most insidious and dangerous and means that you must have a long-term exposure to real assets (equities, property) in spite of the short-term volatility risk

## THE SIX STEPS TO DEVELOPING A FINANCIAL LIFE PLAN

Use the following steps to develop your own plan:

### Step 1 – Foundation

Gather and collate information about your life, the lives of your spouse or partner, and your finances. This data becomes the foundation of your plan.

Draw a clear picture of where you stand in the world. Identify the strengths and opportunities and identify areas of weakness and potential threats. Opportunities and threats generally come from the outside world whilst strengths and weaknesses are internal. Look at how strengths can be used to build on opportunities and to neutralise weaknesses and threats.

Work out your Unique Brilliance Zone.

Draw up financial statements of your current situation. Your balance sheet will show your assets, liabilities and net worth. Your cash flow statement will show your income and expenditure. Use a spreadsheet to project these into the future. Note what this tells you about your ability to achieve important life goals quickly and efficiently, and to be financially secure in the longer term.

Put in place systems to measure your time and money expenditure.

Analyse your insurance requirements and assess the ability of existing policies to meet those requirements. Look at your pensions, and assess likely benefits at retirement. Look at your tax situation, identifying potential future liabilities and checking you are paying the correct amount of tax. Review your wills and the distribution of your estates on your deaths, both premature and at the end of your life expectancy.

Dealing with the unexpected.....!!

**Step 2 – Utopia**

What do you want your future life to look like? Complete the exercises and answer the questions set out in the chapter on self-discovery. List important personal projects. Add detail by painting a word or actual picture of your future life. Set out a time line of when you want to achieve specific goals.

Have conversations with your spouse or partner, family and friends, colleagues at work, your professional or spiritual connections, to help you formulate your goals. Ideas take time, and if you are having difficulty in setting goals you may want to simply plan to take more time to plan in the first instance.

Start to cost these out so you can put them into your lifetime cash flow. Remember that to be able to live a normal life from day-to-day is itself a personal project, and needs to be costed out. You may decide you wish to live more frugally or more extravagantly, or stay as you are.

Don't forget your own personal development, your mind, body, spirit, and the costs of travel with a purpose.

## Step 3 – Transformation

This is about moving from where you are now to where you want to be, and addressing the obstacles. Obstacles may be practical, financial and emotional, internal and external. Your plan begins to form around your solutions to these obstacles.

If you find yourself using the word 'but' in your speech or writing, try replacing it with the word 'and' and see how your mind set shifts.

Emotional or internal obstacles, fear especially, are often greater than practical or financial obstacles, so be imaginative and creative in your approach. Don't be afraid to ask for help and build up a professional support team to help you; this may include a life coach, therapist, spiritual adviser, careers adviser, business coach as well as a financial planner, accountant and solicitor.

**Step 4 – Utilisation of resources**

Your main resources are financial. Use your lifetime cash flow and the cascade model to adjust the allocation to the various asset classes to balance inflation neutralising growth and volatility neutralising liquidity. Use tax-privileged investment vehicles to reduce tax. Check that other financial products such as mortgages and life assurance still do what you want efficiently and cheaply.

Look at your other resources such as your skill sets, connections, properties and chattels and work out how best to use them in the furtherance of your goals. Some resources, such as your skills, may need upgrading or further development and it may be worth spending some money on them to make them more useful.

Touch base with your professional support team. Tell them what you are up to, and seek their help where necessary.

For the financially inexperienced, use some of the many resources on the web to gain a greater understanding of matters financial.

There are plenty of resources outside your immediate environment that you can utilise to help you. Many are free, others might incur a cost. The rest of the world, connected via the worldwide web, is a powerful resource, giving access to ideas, education, crowd sourcing, crowd funding, peer-to-peer borrowing and lending and so on.

**Step 5 – Roadmap**

Write it down. It does not have to be a long document, and should include your goals, the obstacles, your plan for getting round the obstacles, the way you are going to manage your resources and the changes that need to be made. Set dates and priorities. Set down (on paper or on your preferred app) your spending plans. Include a personal development or mind, body, spirit plan. Your financial plan will include your projected lifetime cash flow and lifetime liquid assets charts, as well as decisions about asset allocation and financial products.

## Step 6 – Execution

In fact, you have probably been executing since you started the process. Even as you started to measure your situation in the foundation phase, you probably made changes. Realising how much you were spending on electricity might have made you more diligent about switching out the lights or changing your electricity supplier.

Don't expect it all to happen at once. This is an iterative process during which you will often go back to your plans, review them, adjust them, revise them. Execution involves living your plan on a day-to-day basis, monitoring progress, checking your expenditure of time and money, not losing sight of your goals.

Execution may be in phases, especially if your start point is one of weakness rather than strength. In this case, you may be happy to spend a few years consolidating and rebuilding within limited boundaries, before moving on to a second stage of real goal achievement and expanding boundaries.

Execution also involves a formal review of your plans, at least annually. Go back to Step 1 and start over. Each time you do this it becomes easier. Your self-knowledge is in place and simply gets deeper. Your goals may or may not change. The obstacles will be being dealt with. Your resource plan probably just needs maintenance rather than full-blown restructuring. Your roadmap simply needs updating. Execution is ongoing.

### Financial framework

A methodical and systematic financial framework is an integral part of your life and financial plan. The following section sets out the various elements and flows that make this up. Personal financial planning is just that – personal, so each individual or family will want to adjust the flows and figures to suit their own specific circumstances.

**1 – Income.** This is your earned or self-employed income. It could also include income from dividends (although strictly this should be re-invested for compound returns), royalties, trusts, state benefits and gifts. If you receive taxable income gross it is important that you calculate the potential tax liability and hold this in the Security Fund until payment is due, say 15%.

**2 – Primary account.** This is at the centre of your financial framework. All your income should come into this account, not your spending account. This could be a deposit or interest bearing account, provided your bank will permit regular withdrawals.

**3 – Security fund.** This is your emergency / buffer fund, probably amounting to between three and six months expenditure, plus future tax payments and planned future one-off payments (e g holidays). Keep it topped up as necessary.

**4 – Loans / loan repayment.** From your primary account, direct 10% of your income to debt repayment.

**5 – Tithes.** From your primary account, direct 10% of your income to charities of your choice.

**6 – Savings and investments**. From your primary account, transfer 15% into savings and investments, splitting this between short, medium and longer-term tranches, with the majority directed towards the longer-term, equity-based tranche, including pension plans. Indeed, if you have no major expenditure coming up in the short or medium term, these two tranches may be minimal.

**7 – Spending account**. From your primary account, transfer the amount of your planned regular spending (50% of gross income) to your spending account that you use for your day-to-day spending. This is an amount you should be able to calculate from your cash flow. A variation is to hold a balance of one month's spending in this account so that you are, in effect, spending last month's income. For couples, this should be a joint account so that it stays open (and direct debit payments remain in force) in the event of the death of one partner.

You may well find this a daunting proposition. The idea of spending only 50% of what you earn is anathema in today's consumer society and borrow-and-spend culture. It is hard work, especially in the early days. Indeed, it may force you to consider whether your current income reflects your true worth.

Whilst maintaining the structure, it may be necessary to adjust the flows and the size of the different elements. For instance, if you are heavily indebted, you may want to direct more than 10% into debt repayment for a while. If you do voluntary work on a regular basis you may see this as a substitute for tithing. If your employer or business contributes to your pension (as is becoming the norm in the UK through auto-enrolment) you may not need to direct as much as 15% into savings. Consult your lifetime cash flow, which should provide the answer to all of these questions.

## YOUR ROUTE TO SECURITY AND FULFILMENT

It is difficult to overestimate the power of financial life planning. I have seen it change the lives of individuals and families, often in the most dramatic way. I have seen clients released from the shackles of ignorance and fear that have bound them into unfulfilled lives. I have seen people understand their true potential and go on to lead lives of purpose and integrity.

I have helped clients to see money as a means to an end, not an end in itself, and to reconnect their lives and their money. With a clear direction and vision of their future I have helped them re-structure their finances to get them onto an even keel and then to flourish.

Well-structured finances and a powerful vision of the future have enabled my clients to weather the financial storms that have prevailed in the global economy in recent decades. Through prudent planning I have ensured that, even during turbulent times, they have had the right money in the right place at the right time to maintain their lifestyle and continue with their important personal projects.

I have achieved this using the principles, planning process and financial framework I have set out in this book. I believe these are not only appropriate for the world in which we live, they are absolutely necessary if we are to take the mature and wise attitude to our personal finances that will provide peace of mind and achieve our profound personal goals in a high pressure, money-oriented world.

Given the threats of longevity, inflation and government expenditure cuts (which in Western economies are likely to continue for many years), this approach will provide a degree of independence and financial security that may be difficult to achieve any other way.

Above all, I believe financial life planning is important for everyone, especially those who feel they are leading 'lives of quiet desperation', as Henry Thoreau put it. There is a giant in every one of us, waiting to get out. Often it is imprisoned by our attitude to money. The way out for the giant is through understanding, education and planning. That is the purpose of this book and I hope it will be a valuable and inspirational resource for you.

'Alas for those who never sing,
but die with all their music in them.'

OLIVER WENDELL HOLMES

# End Notes

# WITH GRATITUDE

This book is the product of years of professional practice, training, conversations and personal experiences and as such I have many people to thank.

My clients have been a wonderful source of wisdom, inspiration and stories. It has been a joy to work with them, often for large parts of their lifetimes and every conversation has been a learning experience for me (and, I hope, for them), for which I offer my sincere thanks.

My fellow professionals have provided a huge amount of knowledge and understanding over the years. Attending conferences and workshops (and speaking at some) has always been high on my agenda and the many talks, Q&A sessions or informal conversations at the bar have always been a source of inspiration and change. Thanks, therefore, are due to my fellow Certified Financial Planners (CM) and to the Institute of Financial Planning in Bristol, the professional body in the UK for financial planners, which has been a constant source of support and learning.

If I were to thank one planner in particular it would be Julie Lord who introduced me to the Institute and persuaded me to become a member, and in thanking her I thank all those planners, IFP members and IFP staff with whom I subsequently came in contact and indeed many of whom have become close friends.

It is often difficult to identify the sources of original ideas in the profession. However, I hope I have acknowledged all the many contributions and ideas of my fellow professions, and if I have not then I apologise unreservedly.

I have to thank those who helped me on my journey from the dark to the light, which began on 13 July 2004 when I attended George Kinder's first *Seven Stages of Money Maturity* workshop in the UK. I will always be grateful to the late David Norton for inviting me to attend this event, which led to an amazing relationship with George Kinder and the Kinder Institute. Over the following four years I attended George's trainings and mentorship programmes in the US, which were as much an opportunity for deep self-exploration as they were about the revolutionary approach to personal finance that forms part of this book. Along with George, my special thanks go to Susan Galvan, Mary Zimmerman, Ed Jacobson and Martin Siesta who helped to run the programmes. They provided the support and encouragement for the deeply emotional journey that helped me to deal with my fears and demons and see my life in a new light.

The small group of planners from around the world who attended those courses were also a huge support, and in particular I want to thank Phil Dyer, who became my planning partner, and Lisa Kirchenbauer. Phil and Lisa subsequently ran the Total Business Transformation retreat in the beautiful Torre del Tartufo in Tuscany. This led to further self-exploration and a deeply revealing insight into my own personal and business direction. Once again, it put me in touch with a number of business owners who became good friends and remain part of my support network, for which I am truly thankful.

Abbot Timothy Wright has been a friend since my teens, and a conversation over dinner in Rome in 2010 led indirectly to Vivien Sabel and whilst I don't think my journey from the dark to the light will ever be come to an end I must thank Timothy and Vivien for helping me make remarkable progress.

If all of these people have contributed material for this book, then the Key Person of Influence Team at Entrevo in London are the ones who provided me with the inspiration and methodology for getting it onto paper, and I want to thank Mindy Gibbins-Klein and Andrew Priestley in particular for their advice, help and encouragement.

Thanks also to Chas and Jane Awdry, Maaike Carter, Nicki Clive, Sarah Corden Lloyd, Kit Dollard, Steve Fenton, Julie Feuerborn, Hannah Foxley (much missed and may she rest in peace), Simonne Gnessen, George Kinder, Lisa Kirchenbauer, Jane Lush, Carol Robinson and Tom Wiseman for their insightful comments on the content and my style. Your criticisms were received with thanks and much appreciated.

I owe my thanks to Clang and Tim Bulmer for working out how to illustrate the book and create meaningful diagrams. Books on personal finance can often be turgid and humourless and Tim and Clang have, I think, done much to help avoid this.

Thanks to Lucy McCarraher and her team at Rethink for getting this out and onto the shelves. I now realise that direction, support and firm advice is a necessity for a first time author, and the Rethink team certainly provided plenty of this. It is much appreciated.

Finally a huge thanks and hugs to Clang and Alex Deedes. If I have not been able to give them as much attention as I should have whilst I have been scribbling away then I apologise and hope they will forgive me for directing my time towards, hopefully, providing my readers with the means to make the world a better place.

# RESOURCES

Here is a list of resources I have found helpful in my own planning and my planning for my clients. I should make it clear that I list these recommendations only because I or my clients have found them useful, and not because I am being paid or otherwise induced to list them here.

## ORGANISATIONS

**The School of Life** was founded by author Alain de Botton and others in 2008. It has centres in Melbourne, Paris, Amsterdam and London (and YouTube). The school runs a wide variety of courses designed to help individuals lead better lives. Some are very practical, such as how to select your wardrobe to reflect the real you, to more philosophical subjects such as the role of compassion and ethics in daily life. Many of the courses start with the words 'How to…' whilst others are centred on the meaning of life. The school runs a 12-month Emotional Intelligence programme covering work, love, self, home, community, meaning and culture. These topics, unsurprisingly, are not far removed from the list of common goals I set out in Chapter 5.

**The Institute of Financial Planning** (IFP) is based in Bristol and is the professional body for Certified Financial Planners in the UK. The institute runs a website for consumers where you can find a planner near you. There are also a range of tools and tips. (http://www.financialplanning.org.uk/wayfinder).

**The Kinder Institute** (www.kinderinstitute.com) based in Boston, MA, is the professional body for financial life planners using the Kinder Institute methodology. The resources section for the general public is where you can find a life planner around the globe (see also the *Life Planning for You* book and website below).

In the USA, the **Financial Planning Association** (FPA) carries out a similar role to the IFP in the UK. It too has a Find a Planner facility at www.plannersearch.org.

**The Financial Conduct Authority** (www.fca.org.uk) is the body that regulates retail financial advice in the UK. You can search on the FCA Register to ensure the adviser you are talking to is actually an authorised adviser. You can also find information on current scams and other health warnings to do with personal finance. A related organisation, the *Money Advice Service* (www.moneyadviceservice.org.uk) is a UK Government initiative to provide 'free and impartial advice' on personal finance.

## BOOKS AND LITERATURE

There are many books available on financial products and a search on Amazon throws up a good selection. There are many, many books about how to get rich (quick). However, there are surprisingly few on managing personal finances, and even fewer on the life and emotional aspects of personal finance. However, here is a selection that I have found useful:

Jacob Needleman was an early contemporary author who looked at money in the context of life when he wrote *Money and the Meaning of Life* in 1991, setting out how money influences our emotional and spiritual lives.

George Kinder has been the driving force behind the financial life planning movement and his book *The Seven Stages of Money Maturity* is the foundation text for anyone wishing to explore their relationship with money in depth. Kinder has also written a beautiful treatise on meditation, *Transforming Suffering into Wisdom – The Art of Inner Listening*, a really useful resource if you find yourself in pain around money.

Kinder has recently co-authored with Mary Rowland, a long

standing journalist and commentator on personal and business finance in the US, a book called *Life Planning for You*, which can be read in conjunction with a website (www.lifeplanning4you.com) to help you design and live your own financial life plan and find your own life and financial planner.

Vicki Robin, Joe Dominguez and Monique Telford wrote *Your Money or Your Life* in 1992. Billed as the nine steps to transforming your relationship with money and achieving financial independence it collected a significant following for its advocacy of the simple living concept. Revised and rereleased in 2008, it is a valuable antidote to corporatism and greed.

Oliver James' *Affluenza*, written in 2007, also studies the connection between money and emotions and challenges us to concentrate on what we need, not what we want.

Lee Eisenberg's *The Number* grew out of his own personal quest to discover how much money he needed to secure the rest of his life. In doing so he learnt that money is more than just figures; it really is about the life you want to lead. It shows how small the world of financial life planning is that Eisenberg ended up going back to Kinder as the only person who could give him a 'quick and dirty' formula for calculating his own number.

The thesis underpinning George Clason's *The Richest Man in Babylon* is fundamental to wealth and happiness. This is not about get rich quick schemes; rather it is about a slow, steady and rock solid path to a fulfilled life and financial security. A definite must read.

More recent books worth reading by finance media stars are *The Total Money Makeover* by Dave Ramsey and Suze Orman's *Nine Steps to Financial Freedom* (re-released in 2012). Ramsey advocates a common sense approach around debt reduction, accumulating wealth and setting budgets (so very numbers oriented) whilst Orme asks us to look at why our fears and shame around money prevent us becoming wealthy (so more emotionally-oriented).

We are now, at last, beginning to see professional financial planners and coaches commit their knowledge, experience and wisdom to paper and I would recommend *What your Happiest Friends Already Know...* by Stephen Brody, *Sorted! DIY Financial Planning – How to get the Life you Want* by past IFP President Jane Wheeler, *The Behaviour Gap* by Carl Richards, *Who Will it Hurt When I Die* by Dennis Hall, *Sheconomics* by Karen Pine and Simonne Gnessen, *The Wealthy Divorcée* by the late Hannah Foxley and *A Widow's Guide* by Anita Gatehouse.

A peripheral selection of reading around personal finance might include Napoleon Hill's *Think and Grow Rich*, *Rich Dad, Poor Dad* (Robert Kiyosaki), *Extraordinary Popular Delusions and the Madness of Crowds* (Charles Mackay), *This Time is Different* (Carmen Reinhart and Kenneth Rogoff) and Erin Arvedlund's biography of Bernie Madoff (to help you avoid falling into similar traps set by others).

Books around life and life planning are too numerous to mention them all. However, Stephen Covey's *Seven Habits of Highly Effective People* is not a book to be ignored by those seeking to improve their lives. A less well-known book (although an equally good read) that covers the same themes from a different angle is *Integrity* by Dr Henry Cloud. Subtitled *The Courage to Meet the Demands of Reality*, it is aimed at those in business although its relevance to a wider audience should not be underestimated.

*Live Smart After 50* is a collection of articles by over 30 experts in every field relating to midlife and beyond published by the Life Planning Network in the US. It includes articles on money, including one by financial planner Elizabeth Jetton, to whom I refer in Chapter 2.

There are many books on change in business academia. However, *Changing for Good* by James Prochaska, John Horcross and Carlo Diclemente is about change in individuals rather than in organisations. Although its foundation is in breaking bad habits, its reasoning and processes are useful in dealing with all sorts of personal change.

For a bit more on living life with integrity and purpose, read *Quiet* by Susan Cain, *Invisible Acts of Power* by Caroline Myss and *The Pursuit of Happiness* by Darrin McMahon. M Scott Peck's *The Road Less Travelled* is regarded as a classic on how to use suffering to achieve self-understanding. As the title makes clear, *Twelve Steps to a Compassionate Life* by Karen Armstrong is a guide for the world on how to move towards a mind-set of compassion and helpfulness. It is worth reading in conjunction with *The Miracle of Mindfulness* by Thich Nhat Hanh. For a more lighthearted description of the road to self enlightenment, Isabel Losada's *The Battersea Park Road to Enlightenment* is a good reminder that all this self-help stuff can be a bit of a laugh.

I mentioned Dan Kenedy in connection with valuing your time and his book *No BS Time Management for Entrepreneurs* makes good reading.

The omission of any other books you feel should be mentioned here is not a comment on their suitability of quality; its just that I haven't discovered them yet.

## WEBSITES

My personal website is www.jeremy.deedes.com where you can read my thoughts on personal financial planning.

Living Money (www.living-money.com) is where I will be making available a range of programmes and events based on this book. You can also read my team's blogs and articles.

www.sandwichgeneration.com is a valuable resource for those stuck in the middle, and www.schooloflife.com is the site for the School of Life mentioned above.

There are three useful psychometric self-assessment websites worth mentioning. These are Myers Briggs (www.mbticomplete.com), Kolbe (www.kolbe.com) and Strengthsfinder (www.strengthsfinder.com), used in conjunction with Tom Rath's book of the same name.

Most of the authors mentioned above also have their own sites, of course, and its usually worth tapping into these for updates, tips and resources.

## SOFTWARE AND APPS

We live in the app world now and care needs to be taken to select apps that truly provide value and help in living life, and are not simply timewasters or, even worse, time-devouring monsters.

Here is a selection of apps I use on a day to day basis that I have found to be really helpful:

*Remember the Milk* is now much more than just a memory jogger. It has become a very useful tool for managing your tasks and organising your time.

*Toggl* is good for monitoring your time expenditure, once you have adapted it to the full range of life's activities and not just work.

*MoneyWiz* is the app I now use for tracking income and expenditure and setting and monitoring spending. It is a no frills app with a good, clean, user interface and fast and easy data entry. Whilst reporting could be a bit more sophisticated, it generally does everything necessary for running a financial plan.

*MoneyDance* and *iBank* provide the same service as *MoneyWiz* with more bells and whistles, not all of which are really necessary although if you want an all-singing, all-dancing app that links everything, then these are for you.

The *Meditation Oasis* family of apps are a wonderful, soothing source of guided meditations for different situations and circumstances.

Google 'How long will I live?' and 'How long will my money last?' for some useful sites to ascertain what's going to run out first, you or your money.

*Day One* is a journal app. More than a diary, it enables you quickly and easily to record thoughts, feelings, recommendations, wish lists, stories, quotes, comments, in fact everything you might need to jot down on paper at any hour of the day or night. Sync it with your iPhone and iPad for all round accessibility.

*Calculator Soup* (www.calculatorsoup.com) has a range of online calculators with which you can calculate figures such as the present value of a future stream of income (useful if you want to put a capital value on a final salary pension for your balance sheet), annuity calculators and debt repayment calculators.

# THE AUTHOR

Jeremy Deedes is the founder of Planning for Life, one of the UK's first financial life planning practices, which opened in 2006 to help clients plan their lives and money together. He has recently launched Living Money, a training and events organisation specializing in bringing financial life planning techniques to a wider audience.

Jeremy has worked in financial services for nearly 30 years, becoming a Certified Financial Planner[CM] professional and Fellow of the Institute of Financial Planning in 1999 and qualifying as the UK's first Kinder Institute Registered Life Planner in 2007. He served as a member of the Board of the Institute of Financial Planning from 2006 to 2012.

He is married with one son and lives and works in Ryedale in North Yorkshire.

More information about Jeremy can be found at www.jeremydeedes.com. Resources for readers can be found at www.living-money.com. Jeremy and Living Money are also on Facebook, Twitter, Google+, YouTube etc.

Lightning Source UK Ltd.
Milton Keynes UK
UKOW05f0300250315

248481UK00007B/89/P